FRONT RANGE
TRAD CLIMBS
Multi-Pitch Routes 5.4–5.8

D1571896

Brian McMahon and Olivia Hsu balance on the Bastille. Photo by Kerry Kells

COLORADO
MOUNTAIN CLUB
GUIDEBOOK

CLASSIC
FRONT RANGE
TRAD CLIMBS
Multi-Pitch Routes 5.4–5.8

BRENDAN LEONARD
and LEE SMITH

The Colorado Mountain Club Press
Golden, Colorado

Classic Front Range Trad Climbs: Multi-Pitch Routes 5.4–5.8
© 2015 by The Colorado Mountain Club

PUBLISHED BY

The Colorado Mountain Club Press
710 Tenth Street, Suite 200, Golden, Colorado 80401
303-996-2743 e-mail: cmcpress@cmc.org

Founded in 1912, The Colorado Mountain Club is the largest outdoor recreation, education, and conservation organization in the Rocky Mountains. Look for our books at your local bookstore or outdoor retailer, or online at www.cmc.org/store.

Takeshi Takahashi: design, composition, and production
Kiki Sayre: copy editor
Sarah Gorecki: publisher

CONTACTING THE PUBLISHER

We would appreciate readers alerting us of any errors or outdated information by contacting us at the above address.

DISTRIBUTED TO THE BOOK TRADE BY

Mountaineers Books, 1001 SW Klickitat Way, Suite 201, Seattle, WA 98134, 800-553-4453, www.mountaineersbooks.org

TOPOGRAPHIC MAPS are copyright 2009 and created using National Geographic TOPO! Outdoor Recreation software (www.natgeomaps.com; 800-962-1643).

COVER PHOTO: Katrina Managan storms the Bastille, Eldorado Canyon. Photo by Kerry Kells

We gratefully acknowledge the financial support of the people of Colorado through the Scientific and Cultural Facilities District of greater metropolitan Denver for our publishing activities.

First Edition

ISBN 978-1-937052-13-3
Ebook ISBN 978-1-937052-15-7

Printed in Korea

For anyone who wants to look for
a little more adventure in their backyard.

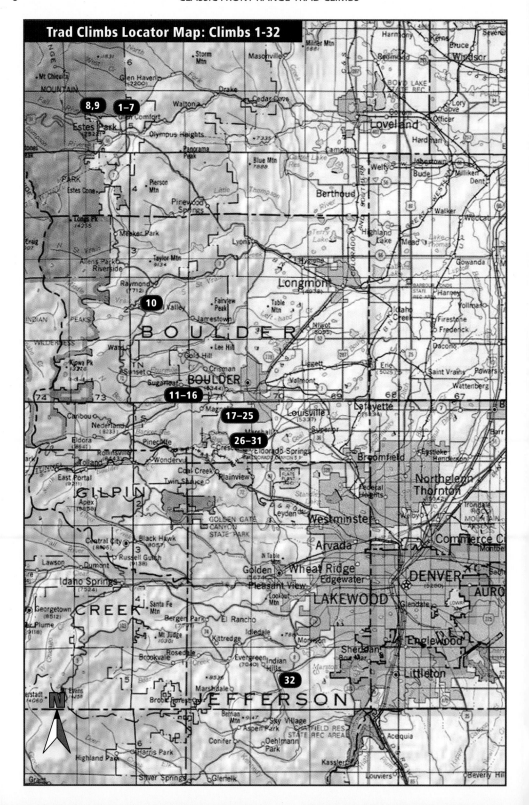

Trad Climbs Locator Map: Climbs 1-32

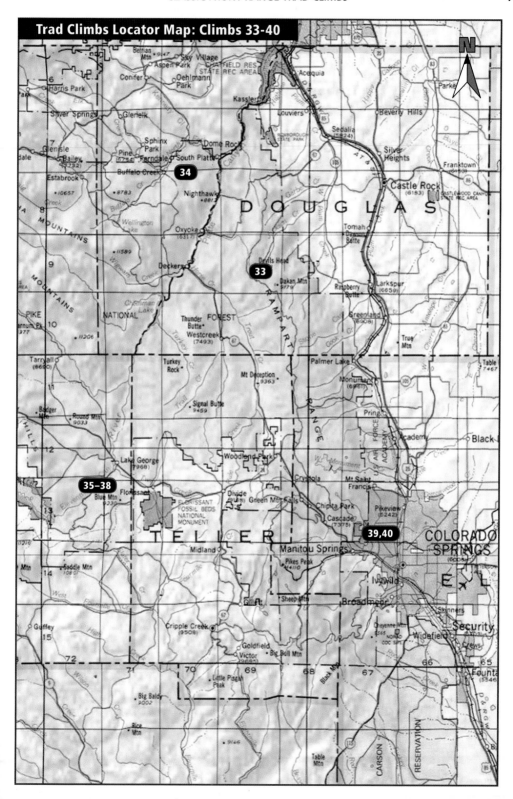

Trad Climbs Locator Map: Climbs 33-40

Contents

Acknowledgements

The authors would like to thank Kateri Ahrendt, Nick Bohnenkamp, David Canova, Wayne Densmore, Mark Egge, Jay Eggleston, Chris El-Deiry, Megan Ellis, Aaron Fredrick, Sagar Gondolia, Abram Herman, Mauricio Herrera Cuadra, Olivia Hsu, Wally Malles, Katrina Managan, Mike Marmar, Brian McMahon, Elizabeth Miller, Cindy Mitchell, Josh Montague, Mike Morin, Hillary Nitchske, Tracy Roach, Dean Ronzoni, Deb Roth, Mark Roth, Micah Salazar, Jack Sasser, Jayson Sime, Alan Stoughton, Heather Teale, Ryan Wallace, Roxanne Weippert, and Brian Williams for contributing photos, and/or their good looks, and/or belays to this project.

Special thanks to Hilary Oliver and Kerry Kells for putting up with both of us.

The authors also would like to thank each other for putting up with each other for not only the researching and writing of this book, but for seven years of climbing (and flailing and often failing) together.

Micah Salazar follows the fourth pitch of the Maiden. Photo by Lee Smith

Introduction

THE ALLURE OF MULTI-PITCH TRAD CLIMBING
By Brendan Leonard

My first year as a climber, I just sport climbed. Then I got lucky and met a guy named Lee Smith, who taught me how to place trad gear and organize multi-pitch belays. From that point on, I was in love (not with Lee, with trad climbing). Something about the adventure of it hooked me: just you and a partner, and a rope and a rack, and six pitches of rock, no line of bolts to follow to an anchor, just your instincts to keep you on-route. Or off-route, as it were. Maybe we'd get to the top, maybe we wouldn't.

In the Front Range, we're fortunate to have more than 10,000 routes and decades of climbing history put up on the walls two hours or less from downtown Denver. I think it's one of the best places in America to learn to lead multi-pitch routes, with the easy slabs of the east faces of the Flatirons above Boulder, the tough love on the tricky sandstone of Eldorado Canyon, and the granite on Lumpy Ridge and in Boulder and Elevenmile Canyons.

When I was a kid, I explored my backyard, then the big field beyond my backyard, then the train tracks behind my friend's house. When I moved to Colorado as an adult in 2005, I got to be that kid again, exploring the mountains in the figurative backyard on the western horizon. I bought guidebooks—one, two, three, then a dozen. I cracked open their covers next to bowls of oatmeal in the morning, by bedside lamp, and in the bathroom. I created a mental tick list: climbs to do next weekend, next month, next year, and someday. And, the someday list keeps growing.

People talk about being a climber and being in love with the movement, the gymnastic control and grace of moving upward on tiny footholds, pulling sideways on a handhold, and holding it all together under the pressure of a potential fall. I enjoy that, too, but what I remember more are the belays on multi-pitch climbs: watching parties inch up the sandstone cracks on the Bastille in Eldorado Canyon from high up on the Wind Tower, watching the clouds bury Longs Peak from near the top of Sundance Buttress on Lumpy Ridge, or watching a blood moon sneak over the horizon from a dark ledge on the Third Flatiron.

If you like the idea of adventure climbing, there's no better place to learn it than here. You can start at 5.4 and work your way up through the grades; and even if you never climb anything harder than 5.8, you still won't run out for a long, long time. In this book, Lee and I have collected our favorite multi-pitch routes, with an emphasis on the longer climbs, three pitches or more. Some of these are easy romps that are great for beginning leaders to practice on before getting into harder climbing (or for experienced climbers to take someone on their first long rock climb). Some will make you question just how hard 5.7+ can be, or tip your hat to Colorado climbing pioneers like Layton Kor and Harvey Carter. And, hopefully all of them will make for good memories.

A UNIQUE GUIDE TO THE FRONT RANGE

By Lee Smith

When my well-established writer buddy, Brendan Leonard, proposed co-authoring a guidebook about moderate, classic trad climbs in the Front Range, I said, "Yes!" immediately. We'd been friends and climbing partners for years, and Brendan often claims I was the one who taught him how to place trad gear and build belays. I think he probably taught himself these skills, but I might have been nearby at the time. Regardless, we both share an affinity for the longer, more fun trad classics abundant in the foothills of the Colorado Rockies. We also love the moderate alpine climbs of the Colorado Rockies, but that's another book altogether.

Every one of the routes in this guide is exceptional for various reasons. None of them are new—most of these routes measure their age in decades. Surprisingly, most of these classics are in a similar state as the day of their first ascent. A few are more polished; perhaps there is now less vegetation and loose stones. But they all offer much of the potential adventure that originally lured the first ascentionists to these classic lines.

This guidebook is unique. Instead of featuring all the routes of a climbing area, this book features a few of the best, most classic routes in several different areas of the Front Range. Route descriptions stand alone, including driving directions and approaches. Find a climb that interests you and go to that page; it's all summed up for your convenience. Although this introduces some redundancy, it helps eliminate needless searching for information.

This approach introduced a dilemma for me. Writing a guidebook is intended to, well, *guide* people. Yet, over-guidance will shortcircuit the adventure aspect of the climbing experience. There's a fine line between NEI (not enough information) and TMI (too much information).

I've roundly cussed guidebook authors for NEI. Many times I've stood staring up at some random piece of rock wondering if I was even on the right planet. One of my personal pet peeves is the domino theory of route listing. To find route "X", simply travel 10 feet left of route "Y." To find route "Z" go down the hill from route "Y." To find route "W," backtrack past the large bush with the dog tied to it... I end up shuffling through several previous pages of route descriptions (most of which I have no interest in) to figure out my route.

However, I believe that guidebooks can, and do, suffer from TMI. If the well of beta becomes too deep, the stream of adventure will run too shallow. You will not find "left foot here, right hand there" information in this guidebook. Hopefully, you'll find just the right amount of beta to whet your interest. Then, find a partner, throw your gear in a pack, and hit the high road.

A climber stands on the summit of the First Flatiron. Photo by Mauricio Herrera Cuadra

Why Trad Climbing?

By Lee Smith

My first real rock climb took place almost 40 years ago, when I was an indestructible youth. It was, by necessity, a "trad" lead climb. At that time, climbing wasn't as popular as it is now, and there was no such thing as climbing gyms or sport crags. Although my foggy memory can't pull up many details about the climb or the route, I do remember realizing, on some subliminal level, that I was engaged in an amazing activity. Jumping out on the sharp end of the rope and forging into the unknown provided escape from real life and sustenance for a growing addiction to adventure and risk.

Fast forward a couple of decades. Enter sport climbing. It changed the world and gave retro-birth to traditional climbing. "Trad" for short. I was partially

A climber high on the Fifth Flatiron surveys the Fourth and Third Flatirons. Photo by Lee Smith

absent from climbing during this time, having given it up for other pursuits. But, climbing had never left my soul, and the lure of vertical adventure pulled me back to the fold. I reentered a much different climbing world: one with bolt-protected sport routes. It seemed like everyone and his dog was now a climber.

The appeal of gym and sport climbing lies in the ease and quickness of pre-placed gear. The climber needs far less equipment and knowledge. In the case of the gym, weather and darkness are removed as well. Climbers can climb faster, train better, and get in more mileage. It's probably fair to say most trad climbers participate in gym and sport climbing. But, ask those climbers their favorite discipline and they'll say trad, hands down.

Why? What's the appeal of this particular throwback discipline in a sport that has evolved into a far more popular and convenient activity?

Simply put, the attraction of trad versus other climbing disciplines is related to the very core of the appeal of climbing itself: exploration, camaraderie, self-sufficiency, knowledge of the tools of the trade, and the ability to overcome adversity with your wits. The trad climber must have a broad mix of experience and skill, a wide range of vision, and a strong resolve to see the route through. The top is often not only a tangible goal, but a necessity for survival. The adventure lies in the uncertainty of the outcome.

Adventure distills down to a desire to seek self-knowledge. Climbers strive against the fundamental forces of nature—the pull of gravity, the solidness of stone, the unknowns of terrain and weather—in an effort to enlighten themselves about themselves. Facing risk on nature's terms, we seek to answer the question, "Am I good enough?" and, "Do I have it in me?" At times we need to dig deeply into our psyche to push through fear and uncertainty. When we reach the top, we feel the great contentment of answering these questions. Climbing is sustenance and escape. It's an affirmation of living life.

How to Use This Book

Welcome to *Classic Front Range Trad Climbs*. These pages contain a sample of some of the best, classic, multi-pitch, moderate traditional climbs in Colorado's Front Range. The routes are organized by area, and the areas are listed from north to south. All the climb descriptions in each area stand alone. The data section contains information on each route: the formation it's on, the number of pitches, the technical rating by Yosemite Decimal System, the gear needed, the best time of year to climb the route, and raptor closure likelihood. There is a comment on what makes the route great, followed by driving directions, approach information, a pitch-by-pitch summary, and the descent route.

Many of the routes in this book were first climbed in the magical era of the 1960s by some of the most famous pioneering rock climbers in the history

Alan Stoughton at the belay atop Rebuffat's Arête on Rewritten. Photo by Brendan Leonard

of the sport: Pat Ament, Harvey Carter, Bob Culp, Larry Dalke, Duncan Ferguson, and The Brothers Briggs (Bill and Roger), to name just a few. Head and shoulders above all, literally and figuratively, was Layton Kor. Not only was Kor a prolific first ascentionist, he was a driving force. He had a keen eye for great lines, and the skills and motivation to surmount them. Some of the best, most classic, and most *adventuresome* climbs in this book were first climbed by Kor. Modern climbers can learn much by studying the history of these early climbing superstars.

By necessity, this guidebook contains many words and phrases unique to the climbing world, and can be confusing to the beginning climber. Many online sources are available to help the neophyte grasp the vocabulary of the climbing world. An excellent book on the subject is Matt Samet's *Climbing Dictionary: Mountaineering Slang, Terms, Neologisms and Lingo.* Another good source, and the ultimate text on climbing and mountaineering, is *Mountaineering: The Freedom of the Hills.* Read up and soon you will be flashing the gnar pumper crimpfest and sending like a boss.

A NOTE ON RATINGS

Go to any climbing gym in America on a Saturday and you'll find 8-year-old kids running top-rope laps on 5.7 routes for someone's birthday party. But, grab the sharp end of the rope on a classic like Kor's Flake, and wedge yourself into the off-width on Pitch 3, and you might curse whoever thought it was fair to rate the climb 5.7+. Such are climbing ratings.

If you're just getting into traditional climbing, lots of things can make a 5.7 or 5.8 feel a lot harder than 5.7 or 5.8, especially if you're climbing high above your last piece of protection (which, let's be honest, can at first be harder to trust than a bolt on a sport route)—or, if you're making the crux move above a spot with ledge fall potential, or you haven't quite learned to trust that hand jam, fingerlock, foot jam, or arm bar. Or, ratings can seem dated if the first ascensionist rated it 5.7 back in the days when a 5.10 rating represented the hardest climb in America.

So keep those things in mind when considering the ratings in this book. Almost all the routes in this collection are great introductions to trad climbing at their grades—plenty of rests between difficult moves; no 160-foot pitches of sustained steep hand jamming. But, sometimes the crux of a route will perfectly illustrate the difference between a well-bolted 5.7 sport route put up in 2005 and a 5.7 trad route put up in 1975.

A NOTE ON GEAR

Throughout this book, you'll notice a "standard rack" is recommended. So what's a standard rack? You're certainly welcome to bring as much gear as you want on any route, but for the purposes of this guide, a standard rack is considered:

- One set stoppers, sizes #4–13
- One each of Camalot sizes .3, .4, and 3
- Two each of Camalot sizes .5, .75, 1, and 2
- Six quickdraws
- Six alpine quickdraws
- Additional gear notes (bigger cams like #4s and #5s, extra long slings, etc.) appear in the route descriptions when relevant.

A NOTE ON RAPTOR CLOSURES

Many of the climbs listed in this book are subject to seasonal raptor closures. We've attempted to note the most prevalent closures in the data section of the individual routes. However, the seasonal closure program can, and does, change from year to year. Four different government entities decide on closures for their particular jurisdictions: the U.S. Forest Service, Boulder Open Space and Mountain Parks, Rocky Mountain National Park, and Eldorado Canyon State Park all have different rules and criteria concerning seasonal closures pertaining to the routes in this book. What does this mean for the climber? Due diligence is required before you head out to the crags. The above entities all have websites listing rules and regulations concerning closures. Heed all signage in closure areas and DO NOT disregard the warnings. Too much is at stake. A closure could become permanent and we might lose access to some of these classic climbs.

Climber high on the Bastille. Photo by Brendan Leonard

1. Rock One Route

BY LEE SMITH

FORMATION	Rock One
NUMBER OF PITCHES	4 pitches
RATING	5.4
RACK	Standard rack
SEASON	Spring through fall
SEASONAL CLOSURES	Possibly closed for raptor nesting February 1 to July 31

COMMENT: Despite its relatively benign technical rating, Rock One Route can offer up a fantastic Lumpy Ridge adventure with a fairly short approach. This approach isn't without its charm; expect a rough-and-tumble tree hucking, boulder surmounting experience before you even get to the base of the climb. ROR's appeal is intensified by a general lack of popularity. There's a good chance you'll have this one to yourself. The lack of traffic on this route is illustrated by the

Kerry Kells on the final pitch. Photo by Lee Smith

amount of vegetation you need to negotiate. Careful consideration is needed to make sure you avoid rope drag. Fortunately, it's very easy to find extra belay spots on this route. Exercise your judgment and pay attention.

Surprisingly, most of the protection on this route is finger sized. You might want to add a few doubles of smaller size nuts and cams, as well as Tri-cams. Although there are runout sections, a selection of smaller nuts and cams will be useful to protect the harder moves. A couple of double length slings and a triple length will also come in handy.

As with most Lumpy routes, ROR has spectacular views of the Estes Park Valley and Rocky Mountain National Park. Take the time while at belays to revel in the splendor. An early fall ascent can be pleasant and colorful. As usual, always be mindful of the weather, as Lumpy Ridge is an electric storm magnet in the high summer. Afternoon soakers are a real possibility.

Beautiful views from high on Rock One. Photo by Lee Smith

GETTING THERE: From Denver, head up to Estes Park via US 36. At the intersection of US 36 and US 34 in Estes Park, take a right on E. Wonderview Avenue for 0.4 mile and another right on MacGregor Avenue. A sharp bend at MacGregor Lane deposits you on the Devils Gulch Road. Another 0.6 mile brings you to a left turn at Lumpy Ridge Road. Follow the road to the parking lot at the end. All the Lumpy Ridge formations are accessed from this parking lot.

THE APPROACH: From the parking lot, head west on the Black Canyon Trail for approximately 0.6 mile to the three-way junction with the Lower Twin Owls Trail/Gem Lake Trail. Take the Twin Owls Trail at this junction (you must climb over a large tree blocking the Twin Owls Trail). Keep your eye on Rock One to the north, and after several hundred steep yards look for a faint trail heading left. This path goes mostly (steeply) up and over slabby boulders to the base of Rock One. Look up for a large left-facing dihedral and a huge left-pointing protrusion to mark the bottom of the route.

Kerry Kells following the second pitch. Photo by Lee Smith

A climber on the start of Rock One Route. Photo by Kerry Kells

THE ROUTE:

Pitch 1: Head up a wide crack in a slabby wall and continue up past a small tree, skirting it on the downhill side. Two cracks present themselves above the tree: take the left one. Slab up to a belay in a small alcove at a right-angling arête.

Pitch 2: Just below the crest of the arête, follow a right-angling crack towards a corner and shoot for the crest before the corner. From here, make for the dead tree leaning against the rock in a gully. Chimney up just right of the tree and find a belay on a big chockstone below an excellent horn (sling the horn for part of your anchor).

Pitch 3: Work the crack just right of the crest of a blunt arête. About 40 feet up, step across a deep fissure to a ledge and move up a rippled slab towards a roof. Go left under the roof and find a weakness to the slab above. Belay on the sloping slab or just past it in the alcove above a steep chimney.

Pitch 4: Find a way through the maze to a 4th class slab up to the very top and belay at two trees. Just look at the view!

THE DESCENT: From the very top summit, head mostly north until you get to easier terrain. Descend between Rock One and the Twin Owls back to the base of the climb.

Topo of Rock One Route. Photo by Kerry Kells

2. Batman and Robin

BY BRENDAN LEONARD

FORMATION	Batman Pinnacle
NUMBER OF PITCHES	4 pitches
RATING	5.6
RACK	Standard rack, plus a few long slings to minimize rope drag
SEASON	August 1 through late fall
SEASONAL CLOSURES	Possibly closed for raptor nesting February 1 to July 31

COMMENT: Batman and Robin is the first Lumpy Ridge climb for many leaders—it's straightforward, and four not-too-long pitches, to the tiny summit of Batman Pinnacle. The only bad thing is that it's closed half the year for raptor nesting. Be sure to check the Rocky Mountain National Park website for access details, or wait until after August 1 to climb. But, once the closure is lifted, it's

Batman Pinnacle. Photo by Brendan Leonard

game on. This climb is a fun introduction to Lumpy Ridge granite. For the first three pitches, you warm up on low-angle cracks and ease your way up to the pinnacle, where you'll make a couple quick steep moves and find yourself on the summit.

Wind (or gusts) can give the last exposed pitch a little extra rope drag, so start early or stay off it if there's a big breeze when you get to the parking lot—or be prepared to haul some heavy rope on the final moves.

GETTING THERE: From Denver, head up to Estes Park via US 36. At the intersection of US 36 and US 34 in Estes Park, take a right on E. Wonderview Avenue for 0.4 mile and another right on MacGregor Avenue. A sharp bend at MacGregor Lane deposits you on the Devils Gulch Road. Another 0.6 mile brings you to a left turn at Lumpy Ridge Road. Follow the road to the parking lot at the end. All the Lumpy Ridge formations are accessed from this parking lot.

THE APPROACH: From the parking lot, hike west on the Black Canyon Trail, past the Twin Owls, and follow the signs to Batman Pinnacle and Checkerboard Rock. Spot a huge square cliff below the south face of Batman Rock, and aim to traverse around it to its left through the talus field that leads up to the slab at the base of Batman Pinnacle. At the base, look up to see a tower on the left, with a left-leaning, right-facing ramp leading up to it—your first pitch heads up easy ground past the far right side of that ramp.

The start of Batman and Robin.
Photo by Mark Roth

A climber follows Pitch 1 of Batman and Robin. Photo by Mark Roth

Wayne Densmore leads Pitch 2 of Batman and Robin. Photo by Mark Roth

THE ROUTE:

Pitch 1: Climb 5.5 terrain aiming up and right of the aforementioned ramp to a big ledge at the base of the next left-leaning, right-facing dihedral. Get a feel for the climbing and protection on these first few pitches—the cracks here are sometimes flared, and gear placements are sometimes a little thoughtful. Don't be afraid to slot nuts in the cracks, or flip a cam around to see if it fits better.

Pitch 2: Head up the dihedral (5.4) to its top and build a belay at the base of two cracks. It's possible to link this pitch with Pitch 3 if you're climbing on a 60-meter rope.

Pitch 3: The left crack is 5.6, and the right crack is 5.7; both are fun and protect well. If you're feeling sporty, check out the right one. Pass a small roof on its left side and climb up to a ledge on the left side of the summit block.

Pitch 4: Make a couple moves up a steep corner off the belay and climb onto the summit.

THE DESCENT: Rappel east from summit anchors to the base of a large tree. Coil up your rope and walk and scramble east to a not-so-pleasant descent gully. One move in the gully requires either careful scrambling or an additional rappel. Continue around the south face of the pinnacle to pick up your packs.

A route topo of Batman and Robin. Photo by Brendan Leonard

3. Magical Chrome-Plated Semi-Automatic Enema Syringe

BY BRENDAN LEONARD

FORMATION	The Pear
NUMBER OF PITCHES	5-6 pitches
RATING	5.7
RACK	Standard rack up to #3 Camalot
SEASON	Spring through fall
SEASONAL CLOSURES	None known

COMMENT: If you're looking for a fun half-day at Lumpy Ridge, you can hardly beat Magical Chrome-Plated Semi-Automatic Enema Syringe, which you might even recommend to friends despite its long and somewhat awkward name. It's five pitches of 5.7, one of the shorter and more merciful approaches at Lumpy

Josh Montague follows Pitch 5 of Magical Chrome-Plated Semi-Automatic Enema Syringe.
Photo by Brendan Leonard

(thanks to its low position relative to most of the other popular formations there), and, in case of bad weather, you can walk off after the first two fun pitches.

The climb itself has a bit of everything: slab moves, liebacking, dihedral climbing, a big roof, and a fun 5.4 pitch that's great for novice leaders for their first multi-pitch lead. The summit pops you out right in the middle of Lumpy Ridge, with views of Sundance Buttress, The Book, Longs Peak, and Estes Park in the distance.

GETTING THERE: From Denver, head up to Estes Park via US 36. At the intersection of US 36 and US 34 in Estes Park, take a right on E. Wonderview Avenue for 0.4 mile and another right on MacGregor Avenue. A sharp bend at MacGregor Lane deposits you on the Devils Gulch Road. Another 0.6 mile brings you to a left turn at Lumpy Ridge Road. Follow the road to the parking lot at the end. All the Lumpy Ridge formations are accessed from this parking lot.

Josh Montague rappels from the summit of The Pear after climbing Magical Chrome-Plated Semi-Automatic Enema Syringe.
Photo by Brendan Leonard

THE APPROACH: From the Twin Owls parking lot, walk west on the Black Canyon Trail and stay left at all forks in the trail until you see signs for The Pear. Turn off on the trail to The Pear and climb steadily to the base of the rock. Find the enormous (30-foot-deep) left-facing dihedral at the base of The Pear. The route begins in a gully just left of the dihedral, in between a 40-foot buttress and the main wall.

THE ROUTE:

Pitch 1: Scramble up the gully, gaining one of two hand cracks (the rightmost one is easiest). Use a long sling on your pro at the top of the hand crack and traverse left to a slender flake. Place small nuts in the flake and climb up through

A pair of climbers finishes Pitch 1 of Magical Chrome-Plated Semi-Automatic Enema Syringe.
Photo by Brendan Leonard

A climber leads Pitch 5 of Magical Chrome-Plated Semi-Automatic Enema Syringe. Photo by Brendan Leonard

a mildly runout slab to the base of the right-facing dihedral above. Belay just above the start of the dihedral.

Pitch 2: Climb the right-facing dihedral to the roof, traverse under the roof, and turn the corner with a welcome fingerlock just above the end of the roof. Continue up the next dihedral and climb the flake, or jump out onto the face to the left. Belay at a left-facing corner. If bad weather is approaching, it's possible to walk off from the top of this pitch.

Pitch 3: From the belay, climb the low-angle 5.4 dihedral up and left for 180 feet to a belay at the base of a dihedral looking up to the route's namesake: a giant granite gluteus maximus guarding the summit of The Pear.

Pitch 4: Stem up the dihedral with palm smears and the occasional fingerlock and hand jam. At the top of the dihedral, walk to the right about 30 feet on a huge ledge to a steep wall. Belay at the base of a blocky, right-facing corner.

Pitch 5: Head up the right-facing corner to a right-leaning crack, placing pro before committing to the tricky-for-5.7 crack. Above the crack, zigzag up corners and slabs to the top. Rope drag can be heinous if you make it to the summit, so an intermediate belay and a sixth pitch is recommended.

THE DESCENT: Rappel 75 feet north into a corridor, then walk east down the descent trail, eventually contouring around the base of The Pear back to your pack.

A route topo of Magical Chrome-Plated Semi-Automatic Enema Syringe. Photo by Kerry Kells

4. Kor's Flake

BY BRENDAN LEONARD

FORMATION	Sundance Buttress
NUMBER OF PITCHES	5 pitches
RATING	5.8
RACK	Standard rack up to #5 Camalot
SEASON	Spring through fall
SEASONAL CLOSURES	None known

COMMENT: Sundance Buttress is the biggest, baddest cliff at Lumpy Ridge, standing tall at the far west end of the collection of granite formations, and seeing fewer climbers than most of the rest of the area because of its "long" approach—which is a little more than three miles. Kor's Flake is the best moderate on Sundance, and is itself pretty stout for its rating.

Sundance Buttress. Photo by Elizabeth Miller

Historically rated 5.7+, Kor's Flake is an old school Lumpy Ridge mega-classic for two reasons: the namesake flake, behind which lies a 50-foot off-width section, and the exposed fourth pitch, where you'll do an exciting hand traverse with a lot of air underneath your feet.

First climbed by legends Layton Kor and Chuck Alexander in the 1950s (20-plus years before cams were invented), you might find yourself a bit in awe at their fortitude—especially in the off-width section on the third pitch. Take a #4 and #5 Camalot to protect the wide section, and even a #6 if you're new to off-widths or just want to sew it up.

Chris El-Deiry at the start of Pitch 3 of Kor's Flake. Photo by Brendan Leonard

GETTING THERE: From Denver, head up to Estes Park via US 36. At the intersection of US 36 and US 34 in Estes Park, take a right on E. Wonderview Avenue for 0.4 mile and another right on MacGregor Avenue. A sharp bend at MacGregor Lane deposits you on the Devils Gulch Road. Another 0.6 mile brings you to a left turn at Lumpy Ridge Road. Follow the road to the parking lot at the end. All the Lumpy Ridge formations are accessed from this parking lot.

THE APPROACH: From the Twin Owls parking lot, walk west on the Black Canyon Trail and stay left at all forks in the trail until you see signs for Sundance Buttress (3.0 miles). As you walk in, look for the overhanging roof on the southeast corner of the buttress—Kor's Flake is just to the left (west) of the roof. As you get closer, you'll see the left-leaning ramp that comprises the second and third pitches.

A climber leads Pitch 4 of Kor's Flake. Photo by Dean Ronzoni

Turn off on the trail to Sundance and head up the steep trail. The route begins at the base of a 30-foot chimney that faces left. Leave backpacks at the base of the route—you won't want to climb the first pitch chimney, or the off-width, with anything on your back.

THE ROUTE:

Pitch 1: Squeeze into the chimney. Sneak under the large chockstone, heading right and emerging on the other side. Scramble up easier ledges to a belay about 50 feet past where you exited the chimney (you'll see the big left-leaning ramp that heads up to the flake).

Pitch 2: Climb the left-facing corner (5.7) as far as you can before it widens out. Stop and build a belay beneath the wide part of the crack, saving any big pieces for the next pitch.

Pitch 3: This is why you came all the way out to Sundance Buttress, whether you like it or not! Some climbers have suggested face climbing outside the wide crack, but if you want to follow in the historical spirit of the route (and use that big gear you hauled all the way up here), get your right side in the wideness and start groveling. Put off using your #4 and #5 as long as possible, but when you do place them, consider leapfrogging them up the crack as you climb. Remember, a couple inches of upward progress at a time in an off-width is enough—be patient. Exit the off-width on easier ground and build a belay on a slab beneath a large right-facing dihedral.

Pitch 4: From the belay, traverse up and left around the right-facing dihedral—when the rock drops away beneath your feet, you'll make some airy moves straight up on good hand jams. At about 130 feet, stop and belay below a roof with a dihedral to its left.

Pitch 5: Only a couple moves up the dihedral here, and you're on easier ground. Run out your rope as far as you can to belay.

THE DESCENT: Scramble right and up until you're on top of Sundance. From the top, walk east to the descent gully. Finding your way down is not so straightforward, as evidenced by the many slung trees in the gully. One or two rappels down the gully will probably be necessary, so have some webbing and rap rings with you. Once you've rapped and downclimbed into the gully, the trail is straightforward, and a short jog to the right around the front of the buttress will get you back to your packs. Return down the approach trail.

A route topo of Kor's Flake. Photo by Elizabeth Miller

5. White Whale

BY LEE SMITH

FORMATION	Left Book
NUMBER OF PITCHES	3 or 4 pitches
RATING	5.7
RACK	Standard rack with offsets and tricams
SEASON	Spring to fall and the occasional winter day
SEASONAL CLOSURES	None known

COMMENT: Not nearly as elusive as Melville's Moby Dick, this Lumpy Ridge classic is one of the best routes in Colorado at the grade. First climbed in 1972, thousands of tradsters have cut their teeth on this aesthetic line. The climb showcases the highly featured grandiose granite of Lumpy Ridge and includes wonderful cracks for gear. Route finding is fairly straightforward and protection is plentiful, although some portions of the cracks can be flared. New leaders

A climber comes up the second pitch. Photo by Brendan Leonard

Mike Morin leading the first pitch of White Whale. Photo by Lee Smith

need to be mindful of the length of the second pitch and monitor gear use carefully. Bring plenty of slings.

Routes on Lumpy Ridge need to be treated with respect. Very often the afternoon thunderstorms descend upon the Ridge without warning and with extreme fury. Keep an eye out for the weather and plan an early start. The Whale faces south, but is mostly in the shade until later in the morning. Bailing on this route can be difficult, and usually up is the best option. Like most Lumpy routes, The Whale has stellar views south to Rocky Mountain National Park. Take the time to enjoy your position high above the Estes Valley.

GETTING THERE: From Denver, head up to Estes Park via US 36. At the intersection of US 36 and US 34 in Estes Park, take a right on E. Wonderview Avenue for 0.4 mile and another right on MacGregor Avenue. A sharp bend at Mac-Gregor Lane deposits you on the Devils Gulch Road. Another 0.6 mile brings you to a left turn at Lumpy Ridge Road. Follow the road to the parking lot at the end. All the Lumpy Ridge formations are accessed from this parking lot.

THE APPROACH: The White Whale is located on the Left Book formation. From the parking lot, hike west on the Black Canyon Trail to a well-signed intersection leading to The Book formation. At the first split, trend left towards The Bookmark, Left Book, and Bookend. At the next trail split, head left around The Bookmark and go uphill towards Left Book. The White Whale starts in a shady alcove at the base of a slabby cliff. Look for a crack that heads up to a rectangular roof with a tree on top. This is the correct start.

THE ROUTE:

Pitch 1: An easy-to-protect crack heads up the slab towards a roof with a pine tree on its upper left side. Climb the crack and slab aiming for the left side of the roof and belay at the comfortable ledge, slinging the pine.

Pitch 2: This is the best pitch on the route and one of the best at Lumpy—one of the best in the whole Front Range. Carefully follow the crack system with great pro, but remember this is a long pitch and you need to save some gear for the belay. Alternately jam the crack, smear the scoops and incuts on the slabby face, and revel in the wonderful Lumpy granite. The crack ends, but gingerly step left to a new crack that leads you to a roof/alcove. Traverse left under the roof and find a belay just over the rib on your left. Congratulate yourself for overcoming the heady moves to get here. Take a minute to absorb the sublime view of Longs Peak to the south.

Pitch 3: Do not get suckered into the black-streaked water groove above the belay. It is very stout, nearly unprotectable, and the scene of some fantastic whippers. Follow the easy ledge system up and left to the large walk-off ledge and belay by slinging a big tree of your choice.

Pitch 4: This rarely climbed fourth pitch follows a wide off-width to the top of the headwall. It also increases the route's rating to 5.8.

THE DESCENT: Walk off from the ledge to climber's left (west). Follow the gully down and back to the beginning of the route.

Topo of White Whale. Photo by Kerry Kells

6. Pear Buttress

BY LEE SMITH

FORMATION	The Book
NUMBER OF PITCHES	5 pitches
RATING	5.8+
RACK	Standard rack
SEASON	Spring to fall
SEASONAL CLOSURES	None known

COMMENT: Although in no way resembling the fruit it's named after, Pear Buttress is further proof that Layton Kor had an excellent eye for classic lines. First climbed by Kor in 1962, this Lumpy Ridge favorite is one of the most popular climbs in the Front Range and rightly so. The start of the route is spicy, the third pitch hand crack is 100 feet of pure, blissful hand and finger jamming, the belay ledges are comfortable, and the views are sublime.

The brilliant hand crack on Pitch 3. Photo by Mauricio Herrera Cuadra

The start of this route will get your attention immediately. Of the three start options, two of them are runout above a landing full of large, exposed tree roots and rocks. There have been many incidents on the beginning of this route and some horrific injuries reported. Make sure you're confident in your abilities for the first 20 feet of this climb and keep your composure level high. The promised land is in sight, but you first have to get there!

The tricky and slightly dangerous start.
Photo by Mauricio Herrera Cuadra

Because of the south-facing aspect, it's difficult to see incoming bad weather while on The Book. Afternoon thunderstorms are a real probability, so an early start is essential. Because of the popularity of this route, it's best to do it on a weekday to avoid crowds.

GETTING THERE: From Denver, head up to Estes Park via US 36. At the intersection of US 36 and US 34 in Estes Park, take a right on E. Wonderview Avenue for 0.4 mile and another right on MacGregor

The cave exit. Photo by Mauricio Herrera Cuadra

Avenue. A sharp bend at MacGregor Lane deposits you on the Devils Gulch Road. Another 0.6 mile brings you to a left turn at Lumpy Ridge Road. Follow the road to the parking lot at the end. All the Lumpy Ridge formations are accessed from this parking lot.

THE APPROACH: From the Twin Owls parking lot, walk west on the Black Canyon Trail and stay left at all forks in the trail until you see signs for The Book. Head up the well-worn trail trending east towards the right side of The Book formation, past a distinctive wall with a series of cracks (the "pages" of The Book). Pear Buttress starts on the slab just after a broken section, next to a tree with many exposed roots.

THE ROUTE:

Pitch 1: There are three ways to start the first pitch. The standard start takes the slab (5.7) directly right of a large flake. Head up the slab and traverse left to the flake at the best opportunity. Or, one can head directly up the corner made by the flake (5.9). Both of these starts involve runout climbing above a VERY bad landing. The third and safest way is to stay left of the big flake and climb the easy broken terrain to the top of the flake. This option is considered off route. Whichever way you start the pitch, once you get to the top of the flake, head up cracks to a belay at a small ledge.

Pitch 2: Trend left off the belay to the very edge of the face. At this point you are on the upper side of the Howling Winds Buttress and you'll understand how it got its name. Continue up a crack to a very nice belay ledge. There may be some fixed pro here; the wise will back it up.

Pitch 3: This is the reason Pear Buttress is a 4-star route. Follow your nose up the perfect hand/fingers crack for 100 feet. This is undoubtedly one of the best 5.8 hand cracks in the Front Range. Continue up and right under a small roof to a comfortable ledge.

Pitch 4: Easier terrain takes you up and slightly right into an alcove under a roof—"the cave."

Pitch 5: There are two main ways to exit the cave, both 5.7. Tackle the roof head on, or traverse out to the right and up. Both of these exits look slightly improbable from below.

THE DESCENT: From the ledge above the cave exit, head east and downclimb a groove. Trend southeast to walking terrain. Contour the base back to the start of the climb.

Topo of Pear Buttress. Photo by Kerry Kells

7. The 37th Cog in Melvin's Wheel (aka "Melvin's Wheel")

BY BRENDAN LEONARD

FORMATION	The Bookmark
NUMBER OF PITCHES	3 pitches
RATING	5.8
RACK	Standard rack to #4
SEASON	Spring through fall
SEASONAL CLOSURES	None known

COMMENT: You don't hear the phrase "Lumpy Ridge Splitter" very often for a reason—there aren't a lot of beautiful Yosemite-esque hand and finger cracks at Lumpy. The second pitch of Melvin's Wheel is about as wonderful as it gets, though: a slightly flaring, somewhat leaned-back finger crack that, if not the

Hilary Oliver follows Pitch 1 of the 37th Cog in Melvin's Wheel. Photo by Brendan Leonard

A climber leads Pitch 1 of the 37th Cog in Melvin's Wheel.

Photo by Mauricio Herrera Cuadra

A climber gets ready to follow Pitch 2 of the 37th Cog in Melvin's Wheel.

Photo by Mauricio Herrera Cuadra

most secure climbing, at least takes great pro. It shoots straight up for almost 100 feet, and after you climb it, you'll wish there were more pitches like it at Lumpy.

Bring extra nuts and finger-sized pieces if you want to sew it up. Some parties choose to rappel after the second pitch and avoid the wider climbing above. If you elect to do this, be warned that the crack pinches down to the perfect width to bite down on a rope and trap it in the crack, right at the top.

GETTING THERE: From Denver, head up to Estes Park via US 36. At the intersection of US 36 and US 34 in Estes Park, take a right on E. Wonderview Avenue for 0.4 mile and another right on MacGregor Avenue. A sharp bend at MacGregor Lane deposits you on the Devils Gulch Road. Another 0.6 mile brings you to a left turn at Lumpy Ridge Road. Follow the road to the parking lot at the end. All the Lumpy Ridge formations are accessed from this parking lot.

THE APPROACH: From the parking lot, hike west on the Black Canyon Trail to a well-signed intersection leading to The Book formation. At the first split trend left towards The Bookmark, Left Book, and Bookend. At the next trail split, head

Hilary Oliver follows Pitch 2 of the 37th Cog in Melvin's Wheel.

Photo by Brendan Leonard

left to The Bookmark, the smaller cliff leaning against the bottom of Left Book. The climb begins in a left-facing obtuse corner; a large tree is growing out of the crack just a few feet up. Scramble up to the comfy belay ledge just under the tree—the first pitch is a long one.

THE ROUTE:

Pitch 1: Climb the left-facing corner on good holds and stemming moves towards the two bushes about 120 feet up. Save a #3 to protect the roof just above the two bushes, and then turn it on the right side on fun jams. Traverse right to a spacious ledge with a two-bolt belay.

Pitch 2: The business. You'll either love or hate this pitch. Jam hands, fingers, and toes up the crack, sewing it up with gear as you go. The lack of holds on the slab next to the crack forces you to use (or develop in a hurry) your Lumpy crack technique (hands and feet in the crack), but if you're insecure, just relax and place as much gear as you can on your way up. There's no cheating this one, but keeping the distance between you and your last piece short can make it a little less anxiety-inducing. Belay at a horn under the big roof.

Pitch 3: Climb the wide, flaring crack above, using your #3 to protect. After a bouldery crux, the climbing eases off to the slab above, leading to the summit.

THE DESCENT: Scramble to the northwest corner of the formation and find the rap anchor—two bolts with chains. An almost 30-meter rappel will bring you to a chockstone with slings (bring slings or cord to back this up if necessary), for one more 30-meter rappel to the base of Left Book. Hike downhill and east back to your packs at the base of The Bookmark.

A route topo of the 37th Cog in Melvin's Wheel. Photo by Kerry Kells

8. Nun's Buttress

BY LEE SMITH

FORMATION	Deer Mountain
NUMBER OF PITCHES	4 or 5 pitches
RATING	5.8
RACK	Standard rack
SEASON	Late spring to fall
SEASONAL CLOSURES	Possibly closed for raptor nesting February 1 to July 31

COMMENT: From many vantage points on Fall River Road in Estes Park, the climber's eye is drawn to the remarkable chunk of rock on Deer Mountain, and specifically to the aesthetic line that runs directly up the proud arête of the Deer Mountain Buttress, neatly splitting the face. Nun's Buttress is closer to being an alpine climb than a pure rock climb considering its long bushwhack

Chris El-Deiry follows the first pitch. Photo by Brendan Leonard

approach, elevation, situation, and commitment. Still, excellent rock, beautiful views, and a fun, challenging day are the rewards for climbers with the temerity to see this one through.

The climbing on Nun's is varied and fun. The first pitch has one of the best hand-sized cracks in the Front Range. The belays are comfortable and the protection is fairly good, although the third pitch has a bit of runout slab to give the staunchest leader a little adrenaline bodge. Since this climb is alpine in nature, it's imperative to keep a sharp eye out for afternoon thunderstorms. Be prepared and start early. You'll likely have this one all to yourself. Remember that you'll need to pay the entrance fee to Rocky Mountain National Park. Another note: it's very difficult and time consuming to get back to the bottom of this climb, so—everything up and over with you!

Chris El-Deiry leads the second pitch.
Photo by Brendan Leonard

Chris El-Deiry leads the third pitch.
Photo by Brendan Leonard

GETTING THERE: From Denver, head up to Estes Park via US 36. At the intersection of US 36 and US 34 in Estes Park, take a right on E. Wonderview Avenue (US 34). Remain on US 34 as it becomes Fall River Road. Enter Rocky Mountain National Park at the Fall River entrance. Remain on Fall River Road as it winds through Horseshoe Park. Near the intersection with Trail Ridge Road, find the parking area for the Deer Mountain Trail junction.

THE APPROACH: Head up Deer Mountain Trail from the junction. After approximately 1.5 miles, the trail starts to switchback. At the fourth switchback head left into the woods and contour around the base of all the rock outcrops on Deer Mountain. It will be obvious when you get to the arête of Deer Mountain Buttress. The route starts at the notch slightly above the base of the buttress. This notch separates the lower buttress from the upper section. The large ledge above this notch is called "the Stagway."

THE ROUTE:

Pitch 1 (optional): From below the notch, one can climb the clean cracks in the corner below the Stagway, but this option is rated 5.10.

Pitch 1 (traditional): From the Stagway, traverse in from left to right and hand jam the beautiful 5.8 hand cracks for a long pitch to a palatial belay beneath a corner.

Pitch 2: Head up the left-facing corner on the right side and find a good place to belay on easier terrain. Look for a good horn to sling for an anchor.

Pitch 3: Above the easy terrain is a featureless slab that is fairly runout and perched dramatically above the north face of the buttress. Take the time to appreciate your position. Trend left up the slab and belay on easier terrain again.

Pitch 4: Increasingly easy terrain takes you to hiking ground above the buttress.

THE DESCENT: The best descent is to hike due south from the top of the buttress. A compass is helpful here. After several hundred yards you'll intersect the summit trail. Take a right and head back to the junction.

Topo of Nun's Buttress. Photo by Kerry Kells

9. Right Standard

BY LEE SMITH

FORMATION	McGregor Slab (Rocky Mountain National Park)
NUMBER OF PITCHES	4 pitches
RATING	5.6
RACK	Standard rack
SEASON	Year round
SEASONAL CLOSURES	None known

COMMENT: The imposing south face of McGregor Slab looms above Fall River Road just east of the entrance to Rocky Mountain National Park, and offers excellent bragging rights once climbed. "The Slab" is just that; most of the routes are far less than vertical and offer climbers an opportunity to practice their slab smearing techniques. Due to the exfoliated nature of this granite dome, slabby blank areas are interrupted by vertical or overhanging overlaps to keep things

Jayson Sime high on McGregor Slab. Photo by Brendan Leonard

Jayson Sime follows the first pitch. Photo by Brendan Leonard

interesting. Vertical cracks in the abundant dihedrals offer excellent protection opportunities.

McGregor Slab is situated high on the side of McGregor Mountain and faces full south, so it can be pleasant and warm even in the winter. However, it's above 9,000 feet and is only friendly on the best days. The Slab is also a weather magnet. Climbers should start early to avoid afternoon thunderstorms.

The Right Standard route has been around for a very long time, and it's unclear who climbed the route first. The very nature of the climbing on The Slab offers ample opportunity to wander around and find your own way to the top. With careful preview of what lies ahead, adventuresome climbers can find their own way up this big rock and appreciate the spectacular location.

GETTING THERE: From Denver, head up to Estes Park via US 36. At the intersection of US 36 and US 34 in Estes Park, take a right on E. Wonderview Avenue. Stay on the main road and head for the Fall River entrance of Rocky Mountain National Park. Just east of the park entrance is a visitor center on the south side of the road. Park here and look UP to McGregor Slab.

THE APPROACH: Cross Fall River Road and head right into a gully just east of Della Terra Lodge. Be mindful of the lodge's private property. Once past the

Kerry Kells on typical McGregor Slab terrain. Photo by Lee Smith

main lodge building, head left uphill and find the climber's trail leading steeply up to the base of The Slab. Once there, head right along the base. Right Standard begins in a prominent left-facing dihedral. If you're heading into steeper terrain at the base, you've probably passed it.

THE ROUTE:

Pitch 1: Climb the left-facing dihedral and skirt the small roof to the left. Trend right to a ledge with trees and belay.

Pitch 2: Again trending right, head up through mini-dihedrals and flakes and belay at a large horizontal ledge system.

Pitch 3: Another left-facing dihedral goes straight up the face. The climbing becomes fun and easier at this point. Belay at another large ledge with trees.

Pitch 4: Smear up the slabs and overlaps. Exit right on a big ramp below the summit, or scramble straight up to the top.

THE DESCENT: If you exited the climb to the right on the big ramp you can work your way down to the east and back to the base. A better alternative is to go all the way up to the top and bushwhack down the west side of The Slab. It's possible to rappel the route Camel Toe, but it's difficult to find the top of this route if you haven't ascended it.

Topo of Right Standard. Photo by Lee Smith

10. The Ridge

BY BRENDAN LEONARD

FORMATION	Piz Badille
NUMBER OF PITCHES	5 pitches
RATING	5.7 or 5.5
RACK	Standard rack with long slings to minimize rope drag
SEASON	Spring to fall
SEASONAL CLOSURES	None known

COMMENT: The Piz Badille, a towering granite arête dropping down 400 feet to the South St. Vrain Creek along CO 72 north of Nederland, was so named for its similarity (maybe a little imaginatively) to the "real" Piz Badile in the Swiss Alps. Colorado's is much more mellow, less committing, and a fun multi-pitch outing that's mostly 5.4 and 5.5 climbing after a short 5.7 section on the first

A look back at the upper ridge of the Piz Badille from near the top of Pitch 4.
Photo by Brendan Leonard

The Piz Badille. Photo by Brendan Leonard

pitch. The Ridge climbs the Piz Badille's left-hand skyline (best viewed while driving north on CO 72), starting with a short 5.7 pitch directly at the corner of the formation, and continues up to the top for a great roadside mountaineering experience. If the 5.7 pitch at the beginning seems a little too stout, there's a workaround that keeps the whole climb at an enjoyable 5.5.

GETTING THERE: From Denver, drive to Nederland, and from Nederland, drive 18.8 miles north on CO 72 to a large parking lot on the east side of the road, from which the huge Piz Badille will be obvious.

THE APPROACH: Park and walk downhill to the creek and find a spot to ford the creek—there used to be a log lying across the creek that made crossing easy, but as of summer 2014, it's gone. Use good judgment and don't cross if the water is running too high. Later in the summer and early in the fall it will run lower and be easier and safer to cross. (Further downstream, there's a bridge, but it's on private property, so fight the temptation to take the easy way, and help preserve climbing access here.) Hike north through the woods to the talus field at the base of the Piz Badille. Scramble to the bottom left edge of the face where it meets the talus—this is the beginning of the climb.

The view to the south from the summit of the Piz Badille. Photo by Brendan Leonard

THE ROUTE:

Pitch 1: Right off the ground you'll find the crux of the route. Many options exist here, but some breathing, slab technique/faith in sticky rubber, and willingness to find some small creative protection will get you up the 5.7 variation, which stays just to the right of the arête on good rock and passes a small roof on the left. Belay at a large ledge at a two-bolt anchor. If the 5.7 pitch looks a little too committing, scramble left and up a little to do a blocky 5.4 pitch to the same two-bolt anchor at the top of Pitch 1.

Pitch 2: The ridge starts to narrow down on this pitch—stay on it and follow good cracks up a long 5.4 pitch (150 feet) to a big ledge.

Pitch 3: More good cracks along the arête, and another long 5.4 pitch to a ledge below the final headwall on the ridge.

Pitch 4: Follow your nose to the path of least resistance here—one 5.4 option heads up the left side of the ridge and pops out on top. Use plenty of long slings to mitigate the rope drag on this pitch.

Pitch 5: Enjoy the fun, exposed, barely 5.0 scramble along the top of the ridge. Stop to belay whenever you feel comfortable enough to unrope and walk off.

THE DESCENT: Walk off to the east and contour around to your left (north), carefully scrambling down the (seemingly endless) boulder field just north of the Piz Badille, back to your packs at the base of the climb. Take care on your way down—there are plenty of loose sections in the boulder field, and you don't want to send one down on your partner's head. A safe descent can be had, just be patient.

A route topo of The Ridge. Photo by Brendan Leonard

11. Cozyhang

BY LEE SMITH

FORMATION	The Dome
NUMBER OF PITCHES	3 pitches
RATING	5.7+
RACK	Standard rack
SEASON	Year round
SEASONAL CLOSURES	None known

COMMENT: Another classic climb that has seen its 60th birthday, Cozyhang toys with, but avoids, the massive exfoliation overhang in the center of the Dome. The route gets its name from the belay at the top of the first pitch, but many climbers over the years have come to agree that the "hang" is anything but "cozy." The old school 5.7+ rating should also be taken with a grain of salt; through

Mark Roth turns the roof on Cozyhang. Photo by Cindy Mitchell

the years some of the route has become a little polished. This line has some weird and awkward moves on it, but retains its charm throughout.

Although Cozyhang shares the last pitch with The Owl, the first pitch is classic enough to stand on its own. It has some awkward moves as mentioned, and looks very improbable from the ground. The opportunity to challenge yourself and learn some new maneuvers is very probable on this route.

The second pitch requires some tricky downclimbing and traversing, so it's a good idea for the second climber to be comfortable with "downleading." The leader should always be looking out for ways to protect the second climber on this type of terrain.

GETTING THERE: From Denver, make your way by your favorite route to Boulder. Once in Boulder, head north to Canyon Boulevard (CO 119). Head west (left) on Canyon. The official start of the Canyon is the bridge just past where the road narrows to two lanes. Set your odometer here for all the Boulder Canyon crags. The Dome is the first crag on the right (north) side of the road about 0.3 mile above the bridge. Parking is on the south side of the Canyon.

THE APPROACH: From the parking area, head across the footbridge and take the excellent trail up to the aqueduct. Head left here and take the trail that follows the base of The Dome on its west side. Cozyhang starts about 75 feet up the hill to the right of the lowest point.

The start of the route.
Photo by Lee Smith

Mark Roth eyes the final roof of Cozyhang. Photo by Cindy Mitchell

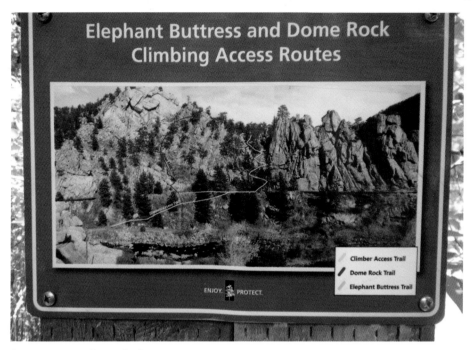

Access routes to Dome Rock. Photo by Lee Smith

THE ROUTE:

Pitch 1: Head for the left side of three small roofs and climb them on the left. Arc up and left on a slab to the cozy hang belay under the blocky overhang.

Pitch 2: Traverse left and down at first. Traverse left and up towards a slot and gain the ramp belay shared with The Owl.

Pitch 3: Go easily up and right to the inverted "V" roof. Although this is the easiest exit, you will again have to remind yourself it is only 5.7. There has been much discussion about the proper way to surmount this roof; most agree it involves wide stemming and an esoteric technique called "head-jamming." Once above the roof, jam the easy crack to the top.

THE DESCENT: From the top of The Dome, head left and down the east side, passing the East Slab on the way.

Topo of Cozyhang. Photo by Lee Smith

12. The Owl

BY LEE SMITH

FORMATION	The Dome
NUMBER OF PITCHES	2 or 3 pitches
RATING	5.7+
RACK	Standard rack
SEASON	Year round
SEASONAL CLOSURES	None known

COMMENT: This classic Kor line from 1959 is a hoot to climb. The Dome's exfoliated terrain offers up some interesting moves on bomber granite, and The Owl will test your technique and boldness like few other climbs. Some claim it's a bit stout for the 5.7 grade; others call it downright sandbagged. Most agree that the leader should be comfortable with the old school 5.7 rating.

David Canova on the first pitch of The Owl. Photo by Lee Smith

The Owl protects well from start to finish, but the leader needs to be mindful of swing potential for the second pitch. The mental crux of the route is the big committing leap rightward to the big horns on the first pitch. The horns are positive, but the move is long and awkward, and the exposure is daunting. This section is a wonderful illustration of the faith early climbers had in their ability to work through any problem and continue a climb. Modern trad climbers need to take this lesson to heart: There's always something better above.

GETTING THERE: From Denver, make your way by your favorite route to Boulder. Once in Boulder, head north to Canyon Boulevard (CO 119). Head west (left) on Canyon. The official start of the Canyon is the bridge just past where the road narrows to two lanes. Set your odometer here for all the Boulder Canyon crags. The Dome is the first crag on the right (north) side of the road about 0.3 mile above the bridge. Parking is on the south side of the Canyon.

THE APPROACH: From the parking area, head across the footbridge and take the excellent trail up to the aqueduct. Head left here and take the trail that follows the base of The Dome on its west side. Skirt the base to the easy slabs below the middle roof.

THE ROUTE:

Pitch 1: Start up the easy terrain to a ramp under some impressive-looking overhangs and surmount the blankish

David Canova cleans gear from the first pitch of The Owl. Photo by Lee Smith

Mark Roth on the "A" roof on Pitch 2 of The Owl. Photo by Cindy Mitchell

Cindy Mitchell eyes the big reach on the first pitch. Photo by Mark Roth

section via a crack to the left. Traverse right above the blank area and look around the corner for the big horns way out right. The move to these horns is a bit intimidating and has given many good climbers pause. Above the horns, jam the steep hand crack in the corner and keep repeating "it's only 5.7, it's only 5.7." After the hand crack, belay on the slab above.

Pitch 2: Go easily up and right to the inverted "V" roof. Although this is the easiest exit, you will again have to remind yourself that it's only 5.7. There has been much discussion about the proper way to surmount this roof; most agree it involves wide stemming and an esoteric technique called "head-jamming." Once above the roof, jam the easy crack to the top.

THE DESCENT: From the top of The Dome, head left and down the east side, passing the East Slab on the way.

Topo of The Owl. Photo by Lee Smith

13. North Face Center

BY LEE SMITH

FORMATION	Cob Rock
NUMBER OF PITCHES	3 pitches
RATING	5.7
RACK	Standard rack
SEASON	Spring to fall
SEASONAL CLOSURES	None known

COMMENT: North facing and shady, Cob Rock is an impressive buttress on the south side of Boulder Creek. It offers several excellent moderate routes with fun movement and great rock. North Face Center is an appealing line straight up the center of the face. NFC is yet another Kor classic from 1959, one of his most prolific first ascent years. It's amazing how these routes have withstood the test of time and still offer great adventure for the moderate leader.

Roxanne Weippert crosses the Cob Rock Tyrolean traverse over high water. Photo by Lee Smith

Wally Malles nears the top of Cob Rock. Photo by Lee Smith

Most of the routes on Cob Rock are very popular on warm days in the summer. The northern aspect offers shade and the approach is short. In recent years, a well-maintained Tyrolean traverse allows climbers to cross the creek during heavy runoff. Make sure you're comfortable with the Tyrolean techniques before you cross.

GETTING THERE: From Denver, make your way by your favorite route to Boulder. Once in Boulder, head north to Canyon Boulevard (CO 119). Head west (left) on Canyon. The official start of the Canyon is the bridge just past where the road narrows to two lanes. Set your odometer here for all the Boulder Canyon crags. At approximately 6.5 miles up the Canyon, turn into a pullout on the left, slightly west of Cob Rock.

THE APPROACH: From the pullout, head east to a Tyrolean traverse across Boulder Creek. This Tyrolean must be carefully inspected before you commit to crossing. Alternately, if the water is low enough, you can rock hop across the creek. Once on the south side find the short trail to the right through the talus up to the base.

THE ROUTE:

Pitch 1: Start in an alcove between large boulders directly below the center of the face. Work the crack systems, generally choosing cracks on the right side. Belay on a comfortable sloping ledge.

Pitch 2: Continue working the crack system, again staying on the right crack. Belay at the comfy ledge on top of the pillar near a deep corner.

Pitch 3: There are two choices: Head right up the harder, flared, hands to off-width size cracks (probably harder than 5.7). This is also the finish for the route on Empor. A much easier option trends left up the deep corner to a hand crack leading to the top.

THE DESCENT:

Option #1: Head south and then skirt around the western side of the monolith back to the base.

Option #2: In 2013 a rappel route was established down the face to help mitigate the terrible erosion problem of the western descent, and it's now considered the preferred descent. However, these two single-rope rappels are very close to the climbing routes on the northwest side of Cob Rock. It's always a good idea to be mindful of climbers below you when you're throwing your ropes for a rappel descent. Most people will need a belay to get to the top anchor of the rap route.

Topo of North Face Center. Photo by Lee Smith

14. Empor

BY LEE SMITH

FORMATION	Cob Rock
NUMBER OF PITCHES	3 pitches
RATING	5.7+
RACK	Standard rack
SEASON	Spring to fall
SEASONAL CLOSURES	None known

COMMENT: This Boulder Canyon classic was first climbed in 1954, illustrating the longevity of these amazing lines. Thousands of climbers have tested themselves on the tricky start and the burly semi-off-width and flaring crack on the top pitch. Like many of the old school routes in the Front Range, the 5.7 rating must be taken with a grain of sand, as in sand-bagged.

Lee Smith on Pitch 2 of Empor. Photo by Brendan Leonard

Cob Rock is an iconic formation in Boulder Canyon and much of the early climbing interest in the Canyon was centered around this monolith. It's a very popular rock and although it has withstood the test of time, it's beginning to show some wear. The routes are becoming polished and slick, and the west side descent has some serious erosion problems. For this reason a new rap descent was installed. As climbers, we need to show some stewardship to these classic old climbs. Respect the rock and the surrounding forest.

Cindy Mitchell on the summit of Cob Rock. Photo by Lee Smith

GETTING THERE: From Denver, make your way by your favorite route to Boulder. Once in Boulder, head north to Canyon Boulevard (CO 119). Head west (left) on Canyon. The official start of the Canyon is the bridge just past where the road narrows to two lanes. Set your odometer here for all the Boulder Canyon crags. At approximately 6.5 miles up the Canyon, turn into a pullout on the left, slightly west of Cob Rock.

THE APPROACH: From the pullout, head east to a Tyrolean traverse across Boulder Creek. This Tyrolean must be carefully inspected before you commit to crossing. Alternately, if the water is low enough, you can rock hop across the creek. Once on the south side find the short trail to the right through the talus up to the base.

THE ROUTE:

Pitch 1: Start at the large boulder on the lower right side of the north face. On the main wall left of the boulder is a right-facing dihedral that's difficult to protect. Above this, climb a flake and belay at a nice ledge on the left.

Pitch 2: Use a slight crack above the belay and trend left at its apex, and move into the large right-facing dihedral. Belay at a comfortable spot deep in the dihedral.

Pitch 3: Follow the amazing right-trending crack (hands to off-width) to the summit.

Lee Smith on the final pitch of Empor. Photo by Brendan Leonard

THE DESCENT:

Option #1: Head south and then skirt around the western side of the monolith back to the base.

Option #2: In 2013 a rappel route was established down the face to help mitigate the terrible erosion problem of the western descent, and it's now considered the preferred descent. However, these two single-rope rappels are very close to the climbing routes on the northwest side of Cob Rock. It's always a good idea to be mindful of climbers below you when you're throwing your ropes for a rappel descent. Most people will need a belay to get to the top anchor of the rap route.

Topo of Empor. Photo by Lee Smith

15. Northwest Corner

BY LEE SMITH

FORMATION	Cob Rock
NUMBER OF PITCHES	2 pitches
RATING	5.8
RACK	Standard rack
SEASON	Spring to fall
SEASONAL CLOSURES	None known

COMMENT: Popular Cob Rock's north face is flanked on the right end by this charming two-pitch route. Back in the day, routes were often named with less flair than today; hence some of the route names on Cob reflect their placement on the face. The Northwest Corner is in fact not only a corner, but a face and arête as well. This diverse terrain demands a bigger bag of tricks than the other Cob routes. It also means the route is less traveled and less crowded than the

Climbers come down in the rain. Photo by Lee Smith

Looking up three Cob Rock routes from the base. Photo by Lee Smith

routes to the left of it. The Northwest Corner is also spicy in certain sections, having a little bit of runout and exposure.

The new rappel route established on the north side of Cob Rock runs very close to the Northwest Corner. This rappel route was established to mitigate the terrible erosion on the standard west descent route (see descent information). When first established, the second rappel anchors were closer to a runout section on Northwest Corner, and several climbers felt this changed the nature of the route. The rap anchors were moved to a different position to restore the Corner to its original character. It was a compromise fostered by the community working towards a consensus—making a more sustainable descent without changing a historic route. This self-policing ethic is part of the stewardship every climber should strive for. The crags belong to us all, but we who use them most have the highest responsibility.

GETTING THERE: From Denver, make your way by your favorite route to Boulder. Once in Boulder, head north to Canyon Boulevard (CO 119). Head west (left) on Canyon. The official start of the Canyon is the bridge just past where the road narrows to two lanes. Set your odometer here for all the Boulder Canyon crags. At approximately 6.5 miles up the Canyon, turn into a pullout on the left, slightly west of Cob Rock.

THE APPROACH: From the pullout, head east to a Tyrolean traverse across Boulder Creek. This Tyrolean must be carefully inspected before you commit to crossing. Alternately, if the water is low enough, you can rock hop across the creek. Once on the south side find the short trail to the right through the talus up to the base.

THE ROUTE:

Pitch 1: Start in the alcove made by the big boulder on the right side of the north face. Gain the top of the boulder as with the route Empor. From here, trend right up a right corner (not the one to the left, which is the route Empor). Follow this corner up the right side of the face and belay at a comfortable pedestal ledge.

Pitch 2: Continue up the arête until you encounter a roof. Turn this tricky roof by finding a hidden and reachy hold. Once over the roof, take easier ground to the summit.

THE DESCENT:

Option #1: Head south and then skirt around the western side of the monolith back to the base.

Option #2: In 2013 a rappel route was established down the face to help mitigate the terrible erosion problem of the western descent, and it's now considered the preferred descent. However, this descent of two single-rope rappels is very close to the climbing routes on the northwest side of Cob Rock. It's always a good idea to be mindful of climbers below you when you're throwing your ropes for a rappel descent. Most people will need a belay to get to the top anchor of the rap route.

Topo of the Northwest Corner. Photo by Lee Smith

16. Bitty Buttress

BY LEE SMITH

FORMATION	Blob Rock Massif
NUMBER OF PITCHES	3-4 pitches
RATING	5.8+
RACK	Standard rack
SEASON	Spring to fall and the right winter days
SEASONAL CLOSURES	Possibly closed for raptor nesting February 1 to July 31

COMMENT: First climbed by Pat Ament and Paul Mayrose in 1964, Bitty Buttress has provided 50 years of fun climbing for perhaps thousands of climbers. But, like many plum climbs plucked during this amazing period of Colorado climbing history, don't expect Bitty to be a "gimme." At the crux, high on the third pitch (where it should be), the protection is a little tricky and sparse. Getting

A climber nears the top of Bitty Buttress. Photo by Mark Roth

off the ground on the first pitch is also difficult, even though a fallen tree adds a few feet of elevation gain not enjoyed by the first ascentionists. Bitty Buttress is classic Boulder Canyon—wonderful featured granite with beautiful cracks and amazing movement. The views are spectacular as well.

In October 2004, a small flare-up occurred with this route when some anonymous heathen installed a pair of bolts near the top of the first pitch. Critics were plentiful and very vocal. The bolts were removed swiftly, restoring the line to its traditional gear state. The bolt choppers made their point clear: don't mess with a classic route done in good style. They claimed that the first ascensionists had the vision to put up a bold line without permanent hardware and the route shouldn't be tarnished by retro-bolting. The community supported this completely.

Bitty Buttress is south facing and can be quite enjoyable even in the winter. It's a wonderful illustration of the excellent lines put up in the 1960s by those lucky enough to be climbing during that time. The crags were wide open with only the easiest lines already completed. Climbing was a fringe activity with very few participants. It truly was the golden age of Colorado climbing. Grab some history for yourself on this fun, stout classic.

GETTING THERE: From Denver, make your way by your favorite route to Boulder. Once in Boulder, head north to Canyon Boulevard (CO 119). Head west (left) on Canyon. The official start of the Canyon is the bridge just past where the road

The start of Bitty Buttress.
Photo by Lee Smith

Looking up the route from the start.
Photo by Lee Smith

narrows to two lanes. Set your odometer here for all the Boulder Canyon crags. At approximately 6.7 miles up the Canyon, turn into a small pullout on the right. A well-traveled trail heads north from this pullout.

THE APPROACH: Follow the trail uphill and bear right at the first fork. Continue on this trail northeast and skirt the base of the Blob Rock massif. Bitty is at the far eastern end of the massif. Head up over a hill and then down to the base of the Buttress. A dead tree marks the foot of the climb. You can flake the rope over this tree.

THE ROUTE:

Pitch 1: The first pitch is tricky at the start and requires some interesting moves. Once over the first 20 feet, this pitch is pure fun. You need to manage your gear well since this pitch is about 165 feet long. Head basically straight up to a very large and comfortable belay ledge. Take the time to enjoy your stellar perch above Boulder Canyon.

Pitch 2: From the big ledge head up and right into a right-facing corner. Stay in the big dihedral, crank over the bulge, and belay at a ledge with a tree.

Pitch 3: Continue up the right-facing dihedral and follow the tapering crack. Resist the urge to head right to easier terrain: it's a dead end. The corner becomes shallow and the crack disappears. You've reached the crux and the end of your protection possibilities for the next 15 feet. Summon your inner calm, head left, and climb the delicate, balancy slab/face to the big ledge above. Exhale and smile. The best placements for a belay anchor are a little awkward to reach. Extending this anchor is desirable.

Pitch 4: This short option is rarely climbed. Head straight up from the top of the third pitch over the overhang. It's reportedly 5.7. Judge for yourself.

THE DESCENT: Descend to the southwest down the gully between Bitty and East Blob. Cut left and follow the gully skirting the base of Bitty and back to the base of the climb.

Topo of Bitty Buttress. Photo by Lee Smith

17. Standard East Face

BY BRENDAN LEONARD

FORMATION	Third Flatiron
NUMBER OF PITCHES	8-10 pitches
RATING	5.4
RACK	Standard rack, plenty of shoulder-length slings
SEASON	Year round
SEASONAL CLOSURES	Possibly closed for raptor nesting February 1 to July 31

COMMENT: Plenty of guidebooks and climbers have quoted Yvon Chouinard calling the Standard East Face of the Third Flatiron something approximating "the best beginner rock climb in the universe." The route is almost 1,000 feet long, a friendly 5.4 (but mostly 5.2), laid-back at a leisurely angle, has six stout belay bolts that have been there since 1931 and aren't going anywhere, a spacious summit and rappel instructions at each of the three rappel stations on the back. How much easier could it be?

A climber free solos the Standard East Face. Photo by Brendan Leonard

Well, don't get too cocky if you're a new leader. The protection on the route itself, similar to most of the Flatirons's east face routes, is a bit few and far between, and if you happen to climb past the belay bolts without seeing them, finding a spot and building a solid three-piece anchor can be a little nerve-wracking. It's also popular with beginners, free soloists, and anyone else looking to have a fun time, which means gear can get dropped, belays can get crowded, and the going can be kind of slow.

Aaron Fredrick leads out onto Kiddy Kar Ledge on the final pitch of Standard East Face.
Photo by Brendan Leonard

But the climbing will ease your anxiety about the funky pro—on nearly any point during the first 850 feet of the route, if you're not standing on two great footholds and holding onto two bomber handholds, you're way off-route. But the holds are so good within a fairly wide deviation of the actual line that getting a little off-route isn't a problem. Keep your eyes peeled for the giant eyebolts and try to stay somewhat close to them. And if you can, get there early (like first-light early) on a weekend, or go on a weekday, to avoid the crowds.

GETTING THERE: From Denver, drive to Boulder via US 36. Take the Baseline Road exit off US 36, turn left onto Baseline Road and drive 1.5 miles west to the Chautauqua Park parking lot.

THE APPROACH: On your hike in, look for the large orange-ish "CU" painted near the top of the Third Flatiron—one pitch of the route climbs from the lower left corner of the "C" to the upper right tip of the letter. From the parking lot, walk up Kinnikinnic Road (the Mesa Trail) south to the Bluebell Shelter and then hike up the Royal Arch Trail to the Second and Third Flatirons Trail. Keep following signs to Third Flatiron climbing access, heading left at a large north-facing talus field before arriving at the East Bench. Take your packs with you for an easy walk down after the rappels from the summit.

THE ROUTE:

Pitch 1: From the East Bench, climb briefly up, then left, across the gully splitting the east face. Clip the first giant eyebolt (but don't stop to belay). Gear is not so straightforward here, but climb where the holds are, and upon reaching the other side of the gully, pick the easiest spot to step up onto the rib running up and down the east face. The second eyebolt is near the right side of the rib—find it and clip in to belay.

Pitch 2: Climb up, looking for the third eyebolt—a more comfortable belay can be built 20 feet left of it, but if clipping that giant bolt eases your mind, go for it.

Pitch 3: Continue up easy ground to the fourth eyebolt.

Pitch 4: Head up and left to the fifth eyebolt, just below the large painted "C."

Pitch 5: Climb up to the lower left corner of the letter "C," then head up and right, looking for the sixth and final eyebolt, near where the rib you've been climbing hits the bottom of the large gash that splits the upper portion of the Third.

Pitch 6: Follow your nose up easy rock on the left side of the gash (don't get too far left of it; you'll be stepping across it on the next pitch). There are no more eyebolts, so find a good stance or ledge and plug in some gear anywhere after you've gone 100 feet from the last belay (or half of your 60-meter rope). A horizontal crack near a huge chockstone spanning the gash makes a nice belay and a good start to the final pitch.

Pitch 7: Step across the chockstone stuck in the gash and onto Kiddy Kar Ledge, a two-foot-wide ledge on the right side of the gash. Plug in a piece of gear, clip a long sling to it, and head up. Sling a bomber chickenhead for protection, and climb up, staying near the left edge of the rock. The final pitch is the technical crux of the route, with a 5.4 slab move near the top. Pull onto the summit, build an anchor over the lip, and bring your partner up.

THE DESCENT: From the bolts on the summit, rappel directly south to the South Bowl and the second set of rappel anchors. From the South Bowl, rappel 50 feet to the next set of anchors—don't zip down too fast; there's a bit of a traverse to get to the proper anchors, which are the leftmost set on the ledge. From the last set of anchors, it's one more rappel west to the ground.

A route topo of Standard East Face. Photo by Brendan Leonard

18. North Arête

BY BRENDAN LEONARD

FORMATION	First Flatiron
NUMBER OF PITCHES	4 pitches
RATING	5.4
RACK	Standard rack with plenty of long slings to minimize rope drag
SEASON	Year round
SEASONAL CLOSURES	None known

COMMENT: The North Arête is a great mountaineering route for beginners because it's got everything but the altitude: easy scrambling, exposure, climbing up to 5.4, traversing, downclimbing, and requires rope management to protect the second climber and to minimize rope drag. The North Arête has all that in four pitches to a summit within sight of Boulder, where you can almost smell your post-climb beer or burrito from the top.

A climber follows Pitch 3 of North Arête. Photo by Brendan Leonard

This is a perfect place to practice mountaineering techniques—slinging blocks for protection, keeping your rope running smoothly on blocky terrain, protecting traverses and downclimb moves for you and your second, and building anchors on a ridgeline where the direction you could fall is not always straight down. Some belay ledges can be a little challenging, so when you stop to build your anchor, think about what direction a fall by your partner will pull the anchor, and what direction you'll pull if you fall leading the next pitch. Be careful of loose blocks—although the First is highly trafficked, a few loose rocks do exist, and dislodging one onto the east face would be bad news for the many climbers who head up the east face

A climber leads the final pitch to the summit tower of the First Flatiron. Photo by Dean Ronzoni

every weekend. Remember to protect traverses along the ridge, even if the climbing seems easy, and set up downclimbing protection so your second can make the move, then clean the gear protecting him/her (not clean the gear, then make the move).

GETTING THERE: From Denver, drive to Boulder via US 36. Take the Baseline Road exit off US 36, turn left onto Baseline Road and drive 1.5 miles west to the Chautauqua Park parking lot.

THE APPROACH: From the parking lot, walk up the Chautauqua Trail, following signs for First Flatiron climbing access. Cross the footbridge at the base of the First Flatiron and follow the trail until you can begin to scramble up and around to the back side of the formation. Stay close to the rock on a climbers' trail as you head up the back, looking for a wide notch with two trees growing at the base of flakes forming the ridge. It's not a bad idea to sling the trees here for

A climber follows the fourth pitch of North Arête.
Photo by Mauricio Herrera Cuadra

a belay anchor for the first moves pulling up onto the ridge—if you fall before you get in good pro, both you and your belayer will go skidding down the east face below the start.

THE ROUTE:

Pitch 1: Scramble through the notch and pull one committing, somewhat steep move onto the face (work your feet high before pulling over), and then climb along the ridge to the start of a low roof that heads down and left onto the face from the ridge. Belay here.

Pitch 2: Climb onto the overhang and continue along the ridge for 150 feet, ending on top of a tower just before a huge notch in the ridge.

Pitch 3: Downclimb into the notch (think about placing a piece as you climb down to protect your second's downclimb), walk across and head up the "quartz crystal pitch," a slabby move with a three-inch-wide pure white quartz crystal sticking out of the face. Head up from that, and continue leftward along the top of the ridge. Cross one more notch and belay on the top of the next tower.

Pitch 4: Climb down into the notch and around to head up onto the summit tower via the right side. Belay from two bolts on the summit.

THE DESCENT: From the bolts on the summit, rappel west 100 feet straight down to the ground. Walk south to the trail between the First and Second Flatirons to descend.

A route topo of North Arête. Photo by Brendan Leonard

19. East Face North Side

BY LEE SMITH

FORMATION	Seal Rock
NUMBER OF PITCHES	5 pitches
RATING	5.4 R
RACK	Standard rack, two 60-meter ropes
SEASON	Spring to fall
SEASONAL CLOSURES	None known

COMMENT: From many vantage points in Boulder, Seal Rock displays its distinctive profile, lacking only a balanced beach ball atop the formation. Gracing the Seal's flank is one of the best scrambles/climbs in the Flatirons. Although not as famous as its longer contemporary on the Third Flatiron, the East Face of Seal is similar and contains one of the best crack pitches in the Front Range. An early morning summer climb on Seal Rock is a joyous experience and rewards you

Climbing a sea of wonderful handholds. Photo by Lee Smith

Climber begins the amazing crack on the fourth pitch.
Photo by Brendan Leonard

with a summit high above Boulder. The standard descent is a somewhat scary rappel off the north side. ***Note: This rap requires two 60-meter ropes!***

As noted, the Flatiron climbs can have sparse protection and Seal is no exception. Most of the lower face will involve runouts on easier slab, with the occasional crack behind a flake or a tree to sling. Look around for pro opportunities and don't miss the horns, spikes, and tunnels that offer natural pro. The belay ledges are comfy and usually come at the end of a 60-meter rope. The fourth pitch is an incredible crack climb with plenty of face holds. It may be the best first-time lead at 5.4 in the Front Range; the amount of protection is limited only by how much gear you can carry. The summit of Seal is a truly wonderful place with the Flatirons stretching out to the north and south.

GETTING THERE: From Denver, drive to Boulder via US 36. In Boulder, exit at Table Mesa Drive and head west (left). Continue on Table Mesa all the way into the foothills and park at the National Center for Atmospheric Research. The Mesa Trail has a spur here on the west side of NCAR.

THE APPROACH: From NCAR, take the spur trail past the water tower to the Mesa Trail. Head south (left) on the Mesa Trail. Approximately 100 feet past the junction of the Mesa Trail and the Bear Canyon Trail, an unmarked trail heads up and west (right) to Harmon Cave. Once you see Harmon Cave (off limits), bear left and continue west up the hill to reach the base of Seal Rock.

THE ROUTE:

Pitch 1: From the very lowest point (or a point up and left about 30 feet), head straight up towards a tree in the center of the face. The correct tree has a nice wide belay ledge. These lower pitches use most of a 60-meter rope.

Pitch 2 and 3: Head up, trending right, to gain the north crest or stay in the middle of the face; either way the climbing is fun slab and a tad bit runout. Trees make for good pro and belay stations. At the end of the third pitch you should be at the Shoulder, a distinctive break in the slab of the East Face. It's interesting to note that after climbing hundreds of feet, you can look over the north side and see that you are only 20 feet above the ground.

Pitch 4: It really doesn't get much better than this. Look left on the much steeper face to find the immaculate crack and head up it. The protection is limited only by your rack size. Most of the pieces you will place are finger sized. Face holds are plentiful. A short crux can be bypassed on the right, or head straight up with a little greater difficulty (5.6). An old fixed pin sits near the top of this pitch. A good belay can be made next to a big flake and a small tunnel that you can sling. Revel in your lofty position above Boulder and the plains!

Pitch 5: A short scramble of 40 feet takes you to the summit. Enjoy the view of the Flatirons stretching off in both directions. It's a terrific spot!

THE DESCENT: The easiest and best descent, and by far the most exciting, is a rappel off the north side of Seal. The anchors at the top of a sport route called Sea of Joy (5.13b) can be found in an alcove about 25 feet below the summit on the north side. *This rappel requires two 60-meter ropes.* It's difficult to get into the rap, and VERY exposed. A good portion of this 185-foot rap is free hanging. Make sure everyone in your party is completely competent with their rappel techniques and fully understands double rope rappels.

Another good option for a competent party is to download the route climber's right to the Shoulder and scramble to the ground. Either way, once down head back east to the base of Seal.

Topo of Seal Rock. Photo by Lee Smith

20. East Face North Side

BY LEE SMITH

FORMATION	Fifth Flatiron
NUMBER OF PITCHES	5 pitches
RATING	5.4 R
RACK	Standard rack
SEASON	Spring to fall
SEASONAL CLOSURES	None known

COMMENT: Bring your slab climbing technique and your runout lead-head for this classic Flatiron East Face jaunt. Although the climbing is straightforward and mostly positive, protection can be very sparse on this route. At nearly 900 feet in length, it's one of the longer climbs in the Flats, and it features a fantastic knife-edge arête in the upper pitches that should not be missed. The summit of the Fifth is a fairly pointy place and the views of the neighboring Flatirons are impressive.

A climber comes up the arête on the fourth pitch. Photo by Lee Smith

The approach to the Fifth is a bit longer than the more popular First, Second, and Third Flatirons, so there's a good chance you may have the whole formation to yourself. It's quieter here, and your climb will probably be accompanied by a multitude of soaring birds. It's best to get an early start since the approach and route are long.

As mentioned, it's very difficult to find protection on some sections of this climb. Both the lead climber and the second should be comfortable with runout terrain. On the upper pitches of the arête, although easier climbing, both the leader and the second are exposed to swinging falls that would be disastrous. The aesthetics of this climb add to the excitement of the runouts, and the Fifth is a summit well-gained.

Rappelling from the summit.
Photo by Lee Smith

GETTING THERE: From Denver, drive to Boulder via US 36. Take the Baseline Road exit off US 36, turn left onto Baseline Road and drive 1.5 miles west to the Chautauqua Park parking lot.

THE APPROACH: From Chautauqua, walk up the Kinnickinnic Road (the Mesa Trail) south to the Bluebell Shelter and the start of the Royal Arch Trail. Travel up the steep Royal Arch Trail. Before you get to Royal Arch, the lower Tangen Tower is just off the trail to the right. From the Tower's western side, the Fifth Flatiron is about 100 feet uphill and south. The start of the route is 20 feet south of the deep tree-filled gully.

THE ROUTE:

Pitch 1: Utilize the deep chimney/crack for 30 feet to overcome the early overhangs, and then step out of the gash to the left. Keep the chimney to your right and swim up the sea of fairly good holds, but little protection. A good belay can be found near an old piton in an obvious crack.

Pitch 2: Follow the belay crack, or the face to the right of it, and slab your way up on more thin holds. Pro is sparse here and downclimbing would be difficult. Start looking for a belay when your 60-meter rope is nearing its end. The best opportunities for an anchor are in the slight crack left of the big gash, although with some exploring you might find a belay in the gash itself.

A climber on the crux second pitch.
Photo by Lee Smith

The general lack of protection available on the Fifth Flatiron. Photo by Lee Smith

Pitch 3: Make for the trees above on a little easier terrain. There's a belay beyond the trees over a bulge at almost a full rope-length from the top of Pitch 2.

Pitch 4: Run up the lower-angle slab to the stunning ridgeline, but don't fall over! Easy climbing goes left up the arête with incredible exposure on both sides. There's a comfortable belay on a spacious ledge just down and left of the arête next to a big chasm.

Pitch 5: Climb (or walk!) up the arête/ridge, over a big chockstone with nothing underneath it, and stop at the high point to take a picture and enjoy the well-earned view.

THE DESCENT: The summit of the Fifth Flatiron has a glued-in eyebolt of the first order. If you read the fine print, it instructs you to rappel to the north for 75 feet. Much of this rappel is free-hanging and descends past wonderfully colored lichen on the rock. From the base of the rappel, head up and around the rock pinnacle due west of the Fifth and head down the faint trail on the south side of the formation. Do NOT get suckered into a descent between the Fourth and Fifth Flats; it's a trap. Once on the south edge of the Fifth, head down (sometimes very steeply) to the base of the climb.

Topo of the Fifth Flatiron. Photo by Lee Smith

21. East Face

BY BRENDAN LEONARD

FORMATION	The Fatiron
NUMBER OF PITCHES	5-6 pitches
RATING	5.5 R
RACK	Standard rack, plenty of shoulder-length slings, plus some cord or webbing for rappel anchors
SEASON	Year round, depending on snow (the descent through the talus can be hazardous if covered in snow)
SEASONAL CLOSURES	Possibly closed for raptor nesting February 1 to July 31

COMMENT: Climbers often overlook the southern end of the Flatirons. I've actually heard people argue that "there are only three Flatirons," which erroneously overlooks not only the Fourth and Fifth Flatiron, but dozens of other marvelous formations. The truth is, plenty of good climbing is to be had south of

Brian Williams follows Pitch 4 of East Face. Photo by Brendan Leonard

the popular Chautauqua Park Trailhead, and as overlooked gems go, the East Face of the "Fatiron" is up there with the best.

At 1,000 feet of climbing, this route is as big as the famous Standard East Face of the Third Flatiron, but a little more adventurous and not quite as consistent, climbing-wise. The approach is longer (closer to an hour and a half), isn't signed, and the climb itself is broken up into two sections: a 650-foot lower section, and an easier 350-foot upper section. In between the two is a rappel off slings (which may or may not be in good repair, so bring your own webbing or cord to rig the anchor with).

The climbing is cruxy and runout right off the bat, so don't make this your first Flatirons climb—it's a good one to do after you've done one or two of the other east face climbs and you're confident with the funky gear and runouts.

A climber leads Pitch 1 of East Face.
Photo by Brian Williams

You'll never find more than a couple parties on the Fatiron—if you see anyone else once you leave the Mesa Trail—so enjoy the solitude on this romp.

GETTING THERE: From Denver, drive toward Boulder via US 36. At Superior, take the McCaslin Boulevard exit, turn left onto McCaslin Boulevard, then right onto Marshall Drive. Drive 4.0 miles to the intersection with Eldorado Springs Drive, then turn left onto Eldorado Springs Drive and, crossing CO 93, drive 2.0 miles west to the South Mesa Trailhead parking lot. If you don't have a Boulder County license plate, you have to pay to park here.

THE APPROACH: From the South Mesa Trailhead, hike on the trail as it meanders west and north to its junction with the Shadow Canyon North Trail. Turn left onto the Shadow Canyon North Trail and walk about 50 feet, looking for a climbers' trail on the right (west) side of the trail, just north of a rock water trough. Head up and west, aiming for the gully north of the Fatiron. A smaller formation, the Fatironette, leans against the base of the Fatiron—scramble around its north side and into the gully between it and the Fatiron to start the climb.

Brian Williams follows Pitch 3 of East Face.
Photo by Brendan Leonard

Brian Williams follows the final pitch of East Face. Photo by Brendan Leonard

THE ROUTE:

Pitches 1 through 3, or 4 (East Slab): Find a crack bisecting the east face and climb up its right side. Set up belays at trees in the crack. After a bulge two-thirds of the way up the slab, the climbing eases. From the summit of the first section, look for a tree to rap into the gully between the two sections (bring your own webbing or cord to back up existing slings if necessary).

Pitches 4 and 5, or 5 and 6 (West Slab): From the gully between the East and West slabs, scramble up the West Slab until you feel you need to rope up—there are plenty of trees for belay stations. The climbing eases on this second section; generally stay left of the line of trees that runs down the middle of the face for the best climbing.

THE DESCENT: From the summit, downclimb to the north and west to a tree just off the summit. Sling the tree and rappel 45 feet to the ground, then hike down the gully north of the Fatiron to rejoin the Mesa Trail.

A route topo of the East Face. Photo by Mark Egge

22. Fandango

BY BRENDAN LEONARD

FORMATION	First Flatiron
NUMBER OF PITCHES	5 pitches
RATING	5.5
RACK	Standard rack with a few long slings to minimize rope drag
SEASON	Year round, depending on snow
SEASONAL CLOSURES	None known

COMMENT: Fandango is a slightly easier, shorter alternative to the popular Direct East Face on the First Flatiron, and the climbing is just as good, if not better and more scenic. It doesn't get the traffic the Direct East Face gets, but it joins all the other routes at the ridge, so expect company on your last couple pitches even if no one else is on Fandango. On a day when parties are lining up at the base of the Direct East Face, it's possible to head a little ways uphill to this

Brian Williams follows Pitch 4 of Fandango. Photo by Brendan Leonard

The start of Fandango. Photo by Brendan Leonard

worthy alternative and both avoid the crowds and pass some of the parties on the longer Direct East Face on your way to the summit. Fandango gives a great taste of Flatirons climbing, and a great sense of scale as you climb up next to the giant left-facing dihedral running down the east face of the First.

Protection is similar to other east-face Flatirons routes, so take advantage of good gear placements when you see them, and be prepared to make some creative belays.

GETTING THERE: From Denver, drive to Boulder via US 36. Take the Baseline Road exit, turn left onto Baseline Road, and drive 1.5 miles west to the Chautauqua Park parking lot.

THE APPROACH: From the parking lot, walk up the Chautauqua Trail, following signs for First Flatiron climbing access. As you walk up the trail, locate a huge ledge system that diagonally bisects the face of the First Flatiron up and right. Fandango begins directly below the left end of the ledge system. From the bridge at the base of the First Flatiron, find a faint climbers' trail (some bushwhacking may be necessary) that parallels the east face of the rock as it heads uphill. You're aiming for a spot about 300 feet left of the bridge: a large flake that turns into a huge left-facing dihedral about 70 feet above the start.

THE ROUTE:
Pitch 1: Climb up to the flake and follow the roof around to the left. A 60-meter rope will not reach the slung tree you'll see after turning the roof, so don't get your hopes up. Belay just after turning the roof to minimize your rope drag.

The middle climber in a party of three follows Pitch 3 of Fandango. Photo by Brian Williams

Pitch 2: Head up to the tree and then up and right, aiming for the huge left-facing dihedral that bisects the face.

Pitches 3-5: Many variations exist from here, and plenty of great climbing with variable protection. Whether or not you choose to stay close to the big dihedral, you will have to join it eventually when it hits the upper ridge. (In the event of nasty weather, it's possible to bail off the back by rappelling from the ridge—but mind possible rope drag: if your ropes are running up and over the ridge and then down to the ground, you may not be able to pull them. Use a cordellette or webbing to extend your rap anchor over the edge.)

Once you gain the ridge, head up and left onto what is known as the "quartz crystal pitch," a slabby move with a Rubik's Cube-sized pure white quartz crystal sticking out of the face. Head up from that, and continue leftward along the top of the ridge, up and down a couple false summits. Plan carefully to avoid rope drag and to properly protect the traverse moves and downclimb moves for your second. Belay from two bomber bolts on the summit.

THE DESCENT: From the bolts on the summit, rappel west 100 feet straight down to the ground. Walk south to the trail between the First and Second Flatirons to descend.

A route topo of Fandango. Photo by Brendan Leonard

23. Direct East Face

BY BRENDAN LEONARD

FORMATION	First Flatiron
NUMBER OF PITCHES	8-10 pitches
RATING	5.6 R
RACK	Standard rack, plenty of shoulder-length slings
SEASON	Year round, depending on snow cover
SEASONAL CLOSURES	None known

COMMENT: The First Flatiron's Direct East Face might be the most popular climb in the Flatirons—a mostly 5.4 romp up 1,000 feet of slabby featured rock, and it's only slightly more difficult than the Standard East Face on the Third Flatiron. When the Third is closed for raptor nesting (from February 1 through July 31), all the traffic detours to the First, so be ready for some company, or hit it early on a weekday or at sunrise on a weekend. Get ready to have a blast. Aside

A climber follows Pitch 5 of Direct East Face. Photo by Mauricio Herrera Cuadra

from the runout first pitch, protection is good—or as good as it gets on east facing Flatirons routes, which means take advantage of good placements when you get the chance. Be comfortable building creative belays, and don't sweat it too much if you don't follow the exact pitch descriptions. The climbing is featured, but runout, and there are probably dozens of 5.6 variations to this route, so follow your nose and don't make it too hard.

A climber follows Pitch 3 of Direct East Face.
Photo by Mauricio Herrera Cuadra

Climbing is possible year-round in the Flatirons, but some descents (like the steep trail at the top of this descent) can be on the dangerous side when covered in snow.

GETTING THERE: From Denver, drive to Boulder via US 36. Take the Baseline Road exit, turn left onto Baseline Road, and drive 1.5 miles west to the Chautauqua Park parking lot.

THE APPROACH: From the parking lot, walk up the Chautauqua Trail, following signs for First Flatiron climbing access. Just across the footbridge at the base of the First Flatiron, the Direct East Face begins at the base of a shallow water gully.

THE ROUTE:

Pitch 1: Friction up the water gully, aiming for a right-facing flake about 60 feet off the deck. You'll pass two huge eyebolts on your right that will be some of your only pro on this runout pitch. Belay at a tree almost a full 60 meters from the start.

Pitch 2: Continue straight up for about 150 feet, looking for an eyebolt belay underneath a huge bulge—stay right of the huge diagonal gully and aim for the blocks with green lichen streaks. Don't sweat it if you don't find the bolt; find a ledge among the blocks and build a belay.

Pitch 3: Continue straight up for about 150 feet and pick a ledge to belay from.

Climbers on the Direct East Face route. Photo by Brendan Leonard

Pitch 4: Climb straight up from the belay and begin to trend slightly leftward, aiming for the top of the headwall. If you've done the first three pitches at 150 or longer, you'll be on top of the headwall after about another 150 feet at a huge belay ledge that could seat 25 people.

Pitch 5: Head left and up around a huge roof, then straight up the gully on the left side of the roof. Belay in the gully to avoid rope drag.

Pitch 6: Continue up the gully to the ridge.

Pitches 7 through 8, 9, or 10: As you traverse the ridge to the left toward the summit, you'll climb up and down a couple of gendarmes, or false summits. Be thoughtful about how you break up the pitches—use long slings to prevent rope drag, downclimb carefully, and think about where to place pro for your second on sections where they will be climbing down or sideways. Think about where you want to belay your second from, as well as where you want to start the next pitch from (do you want to downclimb the first couple moves off the belay, or climb up, etc.) At the summit, belay from two bomber bolts.

THE DESCENT: From the bolts on the summit, rappel west 100 feet straight down to the ground. Walk south to the trail between the First and Second Flatirons to descend.

A route topo of Direct East Face. Photo by Brendan Leonard

24. The North Face, The Maiden

BY LEE SMITH

FORMATION	The Maiden
NUMBER OF PITCHES	5 pitches
RATING	5.6 R
RACK	Standard rack
SEASON	Spring to fall
SEASONAL CLOSURES	Possibly closed for raptor nesting February 1 to July 31

COMMENT: This iconic Front Range formation has one of the most unique routes you'll find anywhere, and is easily the most photographed descent in Colorado. The Maiden is a slender spire threatening to fall over at any moment, complete with a cobra-esque overhanging west face defying description and gravity. The North Face Route spirals around the big overhang, but the rappel

Mark Egge pulling the 5.6 crux on Pitch 3. Photo by Abram Herman

descent beelines straight down to the narrow fin of the western ridge. It's a spectacular nearly 100-foot, free-hanging rappel with a pencil thin target that can be difficult to hit if the winds are up.

The first three pitches are noteworthy for the strange fact that you actually lose elevation "climbing" the route. The West Ridge of the Maiden is similar to alpine ridge jaunts and, although you traverse up and over several pinnacles, you're actually headed downhill. Because of this weird traversing, you need to be very mindful of protection for the second climber; they are essentially downleading. The terrain is fairly straightforward on the ridge, but involves a lot of downclimbing.

The Maiden is a serious undertaking despite the 5.6 rating and should only be attempted by trad leaders and seconds with solid experience leading well above gear. This climb deserves every bit of its "R" rating. Once the summit is gained, the views are incredible, and the climber can look forward to the airiest rappel descent in the Front Range (or Colorado, or maybe the world for that matter).

GETTING THERE: From Denver, drive toward Boulder via US 36. At Superior, take the McCaslin Boulevard exit, turn left onto McCaslin Boulevard, then right onto Marshall Drive. Drive 4.0 miles to the intersection with Eldorado Springs Drive, then turn left onto Eldorado Springs Drive and, crossing CO 93, drive west 2.0 miles to the South Mesa Trailhead. If you don't have a Boulder County license plate, you have to pay to park here.

Megan Ellis under the west face of the Maiden. Photo by Lee Smith

Micah Salazar goes inverted on the rappel. Photo by Lee Smith

THE APPROACH: Getting lost in the Flatirons is easy and one should experience it at least once. This is a good approach to practice getting lost on.

Start on the Mesa Trail and travel north to the junction with the Big Bluestem Trail. Head right on the Big Bluestem and, after a couple hundred yards, take a left onto the upper Big Bluestem Trail. After approximately 1.0 mile you will rejoin the Mesa Trail, heading left for another couple of hundred yards to the junction with the Shadow Canyon North Trail. Go right up Shadow Canyon for a few minutes, keeping a sharp eye to the right for an obvious but unmarked trail. This trail leads to an old quarry. From here, head steeply up to the east end of the now visible Maiden.

Follow the steep trail on the southern flank of the Maiden. It will be obvious where the rappel from the Crow's Nest ends (see route/descent information). Leave your packs here and gear up for the climb. Continue uphill to the west. At a seemingly impassable cul-de-sac you have two options: climb up the bulging overhang via a diagonal chimney on the left, or sneak through the squeeze cave on the far left (south end) of the cul-de-sac. Continue uphill to the obvious slab beginning of the West Ridge.

THE ROUTE:

Pitch 1: Get your slab on for the 40-foot start of the West Ridge. The climbing here is easy, but completely unprotectable. Belay at the big ledge on top of the slab and look east (and mostly down) at your future.

Pitch 2: Traverse up and down the ridge leaving pro for your second. You'll reach the eyebolt anchor at the base of the huge overhanging west face. This is the famous Crow's Nest. From here it's an easy single rope rap to the ground, should the weather threaten.

Pitch 3: This short pitch heads north and down from the Crow's Nest to belay at a pine tree.

Pitch 4: Traverse left to a short corner and skirt it on the left. Traverse to a large ledge and belay on gear.

Pitch 5: Head up a wide, right-facing corner and gain the slabby, easy east face to the top. Breathe a sigh of relief.

THE DESCENT: From a bolted anchor on the west side of the summit, step backwards into one of the most exhilarating free rappels in Colorado. The Crow's Nest looks tiny on the ridge below. A single 60-meter rap gets you to the eyebolt anchor at the Crow's Nest. Another single 60-meter rap gets you to the base. Make sure your rope really is 60 meters long before attempting these rappels.

Topo of the Maiden. Photo by Lee Smith

25. The North Face, The Matron

BY LEE SMITH

FORMATION	The Matron
NUMBER OF PITCHES	3 or 4 pitches
RATING	5.6
RACK	Standard rack
SEASON	Late spring to fall
SEASONAL CLOSURES	Possibly closed for raptor nesting February 1 to July 31

COMMENT: This stately formation in the southern section of the Flatirons has been a playground for climbers for over 60 years! Perhaps only the First, Second, and Third Flatirons have as long a history. The hike out to the Matron is longer than most Flatiron climbs, and since it is in the southern section, it's less crowded than its northern kin. The shady north side of the formation is cooler

The Matron from the trail. Photo by Lee Smith

and more inviting on summer days, but the remainder of the route up the east side will be in direct sunlight until later in the afternoon.

This climb has two distinct characters. The northern aspect is steeper than the east side. It has more cracks and flakes, and even an overhang to contend with. Add in some vegetation, loose blocks, and a shady, dark belay spot and this section feels more like an alpine climb. But, once you gain the East Ridge, this climb is all Flatiron romp, including low-angle slab with big holds, sparse pro, and beautiful sunshiney colors. The view from the summit is as spectacular as any in the Flats. So go grab some history and have a blast doing it.

Looking up the route from the start.
Photo by Lee Smith

GETTING THERE: From Denver, drive toward Boulder via US 36. At Superior, take the McCaslin Boulevard exit, turn left onto McCaslin Boulevard, then right onto Marshall Drive. Drive 4.0 miles to the intersection with Eldorado Springs Drive, then turn left onto Eldorado Springs Drive and, crossing CO 93, drive 2.0 miles to the South Mesa Trailhead. If you don't have a Boulder County license plate, you have to pay to park here.

THE APPROACH: The easiest and most direct approach to the Matron is on the Towhee Trail. From the trailhead parking, follow the Mesa Trail for several hundred yards keeping a watch for the Towhee Trail to the left. The Towhee rejoins the Mesa Trail in about 0.75 mile. Follow the Mesa Trail to the junction with the Shadow Canyon South Trail. Head up

Cindy Mitchell on the first pitch.
Photo by Jay Eggleston

Cindy Mitchell chalks up on the first pitch. Photo by Jay Eggleston

the Shadow Canyon Trail until you reach a spot directly below the East Face of the Matron. At a sharp right turn on the trail, look for a faint climbers' trail heading west to the base. Poison ivy alert in this section! Skirt the base on the north until you reach a large boulder that is flat on top. Chimney the left side of the boulder and begin the route on the top.

THE ROUTE:

Pitch 1: Follow the best left-angling crack up and burl your way over the crux overhang. Follow a flake to a ledge with a tree.

Pitch 2: Jump onto the finger crack next to the tree and gain another short face to get onto the East Face. Some folks continue on up the East Face, others belay here. If you continue, keep a sharp eye out for a belay spot.

Pitch 3/4: Stay on the right side of the East Face and romp up the easier terrain with difficult-to-find protection. A short headwall leads to the summit.

THE DESCENT: Rappel approximately 80 feet off of a bolted anchor on the west side. Go past the old eyebolt. Look for another 2-bolt anchor (cold shuts) and rappel another 80 feet to the ground. Some parties prefer to carry two ropes up the route and make a single double-rope rappel all the way to the ground.

Topo of the Matron. Photo by Lee Smith

26. Tigger

BY LEE SMITH

FORMATION	Wind Tower
NUMBER OF PITCHES	2 or 3 pitches
RATING	5.5
RACK	Standard rack
SEASON	Spring to fall
SEASONAL CLOSURES	None known

COMMENT: According to Disney, "The wonderful thing about Tiggers is Tiggers are wonderful things!" This Eldorado classic on the Wind Tower is aptly named. Tigger starts very close to another Eldo classic, Wind Ridge, and shares the last pitch with that famous route. From below, very large roofs on the right

Mike Morin sorting gear on Tigger. Photo by Lee Smith

and left side of this route are intimidating, and passage through them looks impossible. However, the left roof contains a weakness that keeps the route to a 5.5 rating.

Although Tigger is rated "only" 5.5, the consensus is that it's a little sandbagged. Some strenuous moves on the first pitch, and the roof moves, are somewhat tricky and exposed. Like many Eldo routes, Tigger has its share of loose blocks and rocks. Make sure you're placing pro in solid cracks and be very mindful of what you're stepping on or yarding on.

There are a couple of variations on where to belay on this route. The mindful leader will try to plan ahead to mitigate rope drag. It's very easy to get a rope stuck on this route. Bring plenty of slings to extend protection where necessary.

GETTING THERE: From Denver, drive west to Golden and then head north on CO 93 approximately 14 miles to its intersection with Eldorado Springs Road/CO 170. Drive west on Eldorado Springs Road through the town of Eldorado Springs (making sure to obey the posted speed limit) to the entrance gate at Eldorado Canyon State Park. After paying the entrance fee, park at the first parking area.

THE APPROACH: The Wind Tower is the first formation on the north side of the canyon. From the parking lot, walk a few hundred feet west to the footbridge. The bridge is an excellent spot for previewing the routes on the Wind Tower. From the bridge, head right uphill on the trail that winds through the gully below the Wind Tower. Stay on the trail past the big boulder leaning against the wall. At the apex of the Wind Tower buttress (the Wind Ridge route), head right and down from the ledge at the start of Wind Ridge. Tigger starts a few feet to the right.

THE ROUTE:

Pitch 1: Start right of the Wind Ridge ledge. Follow a crack in a right-facing corner over the lower bulge. Continue up the crack staying left in the right-facing corner. After about 60 feet, belay on a ledge. You can continue up with several belaying opportunities a little higher if you wish.

Pitch 2: Depending on where you belayed, continue up to the ramp below the large, left roof. Trend left up the ramp and pull through the roof on large holds. Appreciate the exposed nature of this position. Be sure to extend any pro to mitigate rope drag. Stay on the right side of the face above the roof and head up to the belay for the second pitch of Wind Ridge. This can be a crowded spot.

Mike Morin happy to be alive on Tigger. Photo by Lee Smith

Pitch 3: You can walk off left after the second pitch, but it's great fun to continue up the third pitch of Wind Ridge. Turn the awkward, difficult roof above the belay and head left to the summit of the Wind Tower.

THE DESCENT: Walk off left from the top of the second pitch or complete the third pitch to the summit. From there, scramble north to a notch, staying on the east side of the ridge. From the notch, find a two-bolt rappel station and rap 50 feet to the descent trail.

Topo of Tigger. Photo by Kerry Kells

27. Swanson Arête

BY BRENDAN LEONARD

FORMATION	Redgarden Wall
NUMBER OF PITCHES	3 pitches
RATING	5.5
RACK	Standard rack
SEASON	Spring to fall
SEASONAL CLOSURES	None known

COMMENT: Swanson Arête is a great 5.5 climb, and would be the perfect beginner route for Eldo—but you have to climb a 5.6 pitch to get to the start of it. That said, above the first pitch, it's varied, well-protected 5.5 climbing for almost 300 feet, with good gear for belays and easy route finding—a great climb for a beginning leader who wants to sew up a mellow route with gear placements. Allow plenty of time for the descent, which can seem like it's more complicated

Hilary Oliver leads Pitch 3 of Swanson Arête. Photo by Brendan Leonard

The start of West Chimney.
Photo by Brendan Leonard

than the climb itself. It involves a bit of route finding, but believe it or not, the descent route covered here is the easiest there is off the top of this climb.

GETTING THERE: From Denver, drive west to Golden and then head north on CO 93 approximately 14 miles to its intersection with Eldorado Springs Road/CO 170. Drive west on Eldorado Springs Road through the town of Eldorado Springs (making sure to obey the posted speed limit) to the entrance gate at Eldorado Canyon State Park. After paying the entrance fee, park at the first parking area.

THE APPROACH: From the parking lot, walk north across the bridge, then head left at the fork in the trail. Hop around or across the concrete pad next to the creek and follow the trail up, up, up to the Redgarden Wall climbing routes. Stay right at all forks in the trail and keep going until you reach a huge left-facing dihedral with a chimney going up it. This is the West Chimney (5.6).

THE ROUTE:

Approach Pitch: Climb West Chimney, almost a full 60-meter rope length of 5.6 climbing up the chimney. Skip the intermediate bolted belay anchors (but don't be afraid to clip them for protection), and belay at a stout tree at the top of the chimney. Beware of loose rock in the upper third of the chimney. After bringing up your partner, scramble up and right from the belay tree (again, careful of loose rock) to a tree belay on a huge ledge at the base of an arête. Some parties may belay on the short scramble to the tree.

Pitch 1: Start up parallel cracks on the arête and stay near the arête for about 80 feet to a belay in a corner just below a tree.

Hilary Oliver leads Pitch 2 of Swanson Arête. Photo by Brendan Leonard

Pitch 2: Climb up the right side of the arête to a bulge. Place a bomber piece at the bulge, and pull through it. Belay at a decent ledge at the base of a dihedral next to some trees.

Pitch 3: Head up the dihedral to a roof. Place a piece under the roof, then climb right into a huge, slightly laid-back dihedral. Stem and finger-jam your way up the dihedral (great nut placements can be found in the back) to the summit.

THE DESCENT: You're not done yet. From the summit, look east to the next tower—this is Tower One. You'll scramble down around its back side to get off. Lower or rap off the summit to the notch between the summit and the next tower, then coil your rope and scramble east around Tower One, then south and west to a notch between it and a small tower. Head to the notch, then scramble west through it and down a gully to a two-bolt rap station. Knot the ends of your rope and rappel 100 feet west to a ledge. Scramble west about 30 feet to the top of the Upper Ramp and find a two-bolt rappel (the Vertigo Rappels). Rap 90 feet to another two-bolt anchor, and then one more rappel to Vertigo Ledge. Walk west back to your packs at the base of the West Chimney.

A topo of Swanson Arête. Photo by Dean Ronzoni

28. Wind Ridge

BY BRENDAN LEONARD

FORMATION	Wind Tower
NUMBER OF PITCHES	3 pitches
RATING	5.6 or 5.7
RACK	Standard rack to 3 inches
SEASON	Year round, depending on snow cover
SEASONAL CLOSURES	None known

COMMENT: Wind Ridge is one of Eldo's earlier classics, first climbed in 1959 by the legendary Layton Kor. Its exposed, varied climbing on the far edge of the Wind Tower—and a strange roof flake to start Pitch 3—make it a memorable climb, and its short approach and relatively short length make it a great after-work climb in the late spring or early fall. If you're short on time or just want to avoid the funky moves on Pitch 3, you can walk off after the first two pitches.

A climber starts up the third pitch of Wind Ridge. Photo by Mauricio Herrera Cuadra

A climber follows Pitch 2 of Wind Ridge.
Photo by Brendan Leonard

Heather Teale profiled on Wind Ridge.
Photo by Kerry Kells

Wind Ridge is one of the few routes to summit the Wind Tower with a quality last pitch, so if you've never been to the top, consider finishing this one out.

Chances are you'll have plenty of company on the Wind Tower—the easy approach and moderate climbs make it a favorite of Front Range trad climbers. Work out a communication system with your partner beforehand and make sure you're on the same page—it's easy to mistake a nearby shout of "off belay" as your partner's voice, so consider using your first names in all communications, or rope tugs for signals.

GETTING THERE: From Denver, drive west to Golden and then head north on CO 93 approximately 14 miles to its intersection with Eldorado Springs Road/CO 170. Drive west on Eldorado Springs Road through the town of Eldorado Springs (making sure to obey the posted speed limit) to the entrance gate at Eldorado Canyon State Park. After paying the entrance fee, park at the first parking area.

THE APPROACH: From the parking lot, walk north across the bridge crossing South Boulder Creek, then hike straight up the rock steps toward the west face

**Looking down the first pitch
of Wind Ridge.**
Photo by Mauricio Herrera Cuadra

of the Wind Tower. Wind Ridge begins at the far left side of the west face in a small group of trees.

THE ROUTE:

Pitch 1: There are two strategies for the first 15 feet of this pitch: a) climb up the dihedral to the left of a big flake, then traverse right above the flake to gain the arête (5.6); or b) climb the flake itself (5.7). Both protect well, but I've always preferred climbing the flake itself—although more strenuous, it seems more straightforward. After gaining the arête, follow cracks up the face on the right side of the arête to a belay ledge sloping down and right.

Pitch 2: Directly above the belay, climb a hand crack that gradually widens to a squeeze chimney (no wide gear needed). At the next big ledge, build a belay with small gear in a cave. Bring your partner up and either walk off to the left, or continue on to Pitch 3.

Pitch 3: Longtime Boulder climber and guidebook author Richard Rossiter called this the weirdest roof in Eldo: Above the belay, grab a huge flake with both hands and do a pull-up—but first consider how you're going to pass, and protect the moves going past it. After pulling through the roof, it's easy money the rest of the way to a tree belay at the summit.

THE DESCENT: Scramble north to a notch, staying on the east side of the ridge as you scramble. From the notch, find a two-bolt rappel station and rap 50 feet to the descent trail. Don't let your guard down on the walk down just because you're done climbing—it may seem trivial, but more than one Eldo climber has lost their footing and had to be rescued off this descent trail.

A topo of Wind Ridge. Photo by Brendan Leonard

29. Recon to West Overhang

BY LEE SMITH

FORMATION	Wind Tower
NUMBER OF PITCHES	2 pitches
RATING	5.7
RACK	Standard rack
SEASON	Spring to fall
SEASONAL CLOSURES	None known

COMMENT: This fun romp up the right side of the southwest face of the Wind Tower combines the best pitches of two routes to make a stellar multi-pitch outing. Generally moderate in nature, this route has a zinger crux through the namesake overhang adding spice and burl. The protection is good for most of

Hillary Nitchske on the start of Recon. Photo by Lee Smith

the route, although the last section of the second pitch has a dicey traverse in a no-fall zone. Keep your wits about you for this traverse.

Like many climbs in Eldorado Canyon, the West Overhang is quite difficult for its 5.7 rating. The roof moves aren't readily apparent, nor are they physically easy. The climber needs to look around and find the best holds and proper sequence to haul the roof. Many longtime climbers have been stymied by this section. Rope management is important through the roof, and the very old (40+ years?) fixed piton must be backed up with your own gear. As a second on this route you'll have plenty of opportunity to enjoy the view of the splendid Bastille while belaying the leader.

Looking up the route from the start.
Photo by Lee Smith

GETTING THERE: From Denver, drive west to Golden and then head north on CO 93 approximately 14 miles to its intersection with Eldorado Springs Road/ CO 170. Drive west on Eldorado Springs Road through the town of Eldorado Springs (making sure to obey the posted speed limit) to the entrance gate at Eldorado Canyon State Park. After paying the entrance fee, park at the first parking area.

THE APPROACH: The Wind Tower is the first formation on the north side of the canyon. From the parking lot, walk a few hundred feet west to the footbridge. The bridge is an excellent spot to preview the routes on the Wind Tower. From the bridge, head right uphill on the trail that winds through the gully below the Wind Tower. A short side trail heads right just before the big boulder lying against the base of the Tower and traverses across to the right-side routes. The start of Recon is in a small alcove on a ledge on the far right side of the southwest face.

THE ROUTE:

Pitch 1: This pitch starts in the small alcove on a ledge above a drainage gully. It's a good idea, although not totally necessary, to build an anchor here for the belayer. Head straight up the left-facing corner over a small roof. Follow

Hillary Nitchske leads the first pitch.
Photo by Lee Smith

Hillary Nitchske rappels off Recon.
Photo by Lee Smith

the crack system straight up to a large ledge below the overhang. Building an anchor here is a little tricky but doable.

Pitch 2: From the big ledge, head up the slab to the overhang proper. There's an old pin protecting the overhang moves, but it's best to back this up. The moves through the roof are burly but straightforward. Once over the roof, continue up the face to a left-facing corner. At the top of the corner, leave a piece of pro and traverse over to the bolted anchor at the apex of a chimney, just past a scoop cave. This traverse is spicy, unprotectable, and definitely a no-fall section.

THE DESCENT: Two bolted rappel stations take you to the ground. The lower rappel anchors are just below the large ledge, near a small tree. Be mindful of climbers below you on this route and other routes nearby.

Topo of Recon to West Overhang. Photo by Kerry Kells

30. Bastille Crack

BY BRENDAN LEONARD

FORMATION	The Bastille
NUMBER OF PITCHES	5 pitches
RATING	5.7+
RACK	Standard rack
SEASON	Spring through fall
SEASONAL CLOSURES	None known

COMMENT: The Bastille Crack may be the most famous rock climb in Eldorado Canyon, if not Colorado—five pitches of 5.6 and 5.7 cracks and flakes rising up the north face to the summit of Eldo's iconic Bastille Tower. The climb starts literally on the side of the road that winds through Eldorado Canyon, and once you're on the climb, you'll know why it's a classic—the climb is steep for

A climber follows Pitch 1 of the Bastille Crack. Photo by Brendan Leonard

5.7+, well-protected, doesn't require much crack technique, and sits front and center on the Bastille.

It's famous for good reason, and popular. If you arrive mid-morning on a weekend day, expect to wait for other parties, and maybe wait in line at the base. A good strategy is to climb on a weekday, or arrive at first light on Saturday or Sunday. Then, enjoy five of the best moderate pitches in Eldo.

GETTING THERE: From Denver, drive west to Golden and then head north on CO 93 approximately 14 miles to its intersection with Eldorado Springs Road/ CO 170. Drive west on Eldorado Springs Road through the town of Eldorado Springs (making sure to obey the posted speed limit) to the entrance gate at Eldorado Canyon State Park. After paying the entrance fee, park at the first parking area.

A climber leads Pitch 1 of the Bastille Crack. Photo by Brendan Leonard

THE APPROACH: The approach to the Bastille might be one of the easiest out there. From the parking lot, walk up the road 300 feet to the west to the base of the Bastille. The climb begins at a set of blocks under two opposing chalked-up flakes about 30 feet above.

THE ROUTE:

Pitch 1: The first pitch of the Bastille Crack is short—only 65 feet—but can be dangerous if not protected correctly. It's not tricky to do it safely, though. Climb up under the left-facing flake, and place protection at the bottom of the flake. Climb the flake, watching for an opportunity to place protection in the crack to the left of the flake—you'll have to make a move to switch from the flake to the crack, and be sure you've got protection in the left crack before stepping over to it. After switching into the crack, continue up to the bolt anchor and belay—a few good hand jams will make it easy.

Pitch 2: Step into the chimney above and left of the anchors, and climb left onto the face to a finger crack, using the crack and face holds. Traverse right under the small roof to stay in the main crack system and continue up the crack up and left to a ledge. Belay at a crack with a fixed piton.

A climber follows Pitch 2 of the Bastille Crack. Photo by Brendan Leonard

Pitch 3: This 50-foot pitch has a couple funky moves and is the crux of the route. Head up the main crack through blocks to a large ramp that slopes down to the left.

Pitch 4: Traverse 15 feet to the left to gain a short corner, then keep traversing left to a hand crack. The climbing here is balancy, but only 5.6 if you remember to use your feet. Continue up the crack to a corner, which leads to easier ground and a big belay ledge.

Pitch 5: There are several options here, but this guide will focus on the easiest: Head up the wide left-facing corner, about 30 feet of 5.4, then finish with easy scrambling for 30 more feet to the top.

THE DESCENT: Carefully downclimb to the south side of the Bastille. Note the pieces of cable used by Ivy Baldwin in his tightrope walks from the Bastille to the Wind Tower in the early 1900s. Make a few interesting moves to climb to the back of the formation down to the wide path behind the tower. Turn right on the path to find the signed descent trail down the west side of the Bastille.

A topo of the Bastille Crack. Photo by Brendan Leonard

31. Rewritten

BY BRENDAN LEONARD

FORMATION	Redgarden Wall
NUMBER OF PITCHES	6 pitches
RATING	5.7
RACK	Standard rack
SEASON	Spring to fall
SEASONAL CLOSURES	Possibly closed for raptor nesting February 1 to July 31

COMMENT: Rewritten is a moderate Eldo classic with two legendary pitches near the top—the exposed hand traverse off the belay to start Pitch 4, and the moves up the sharp fin of Rebuffat's Arête on Pitch 5. Pick the one that sounds more fun and give your partner the other—they're both 5.7, and both spectacular.

Accidents from rockfall and other causes have occurred on this climb and on nearby routes. It's not jinxed, but it is Eldo. The rock is good, but every once

Alan Stoughton follows Pitch 4 of Rewritten. Photo by Brendan Leonard

in a while it's loose, so be mindful. Check your handholds, place good pro, and enjoy the exposure!

GETTING THERE: From Denver, drive west to Golden and then head north on CO 93 approximately 14 miles to its intersection with Eldorado Springs Road/CO 170. Drive west on Eldorado Springs Road through the town of Eldorado Springs (making sure to obey the posted speed limit) to the entrance gate at Eldorado Canyon State Park. After paying the entrance fee, park at the first parking area.

THE APPROACH: From the parking lot, walk north across the bridge, then head left at the fork in the trail. Hop around or across the concrete pad next to the creek and follow the trail up, up, up to the Redgarden Wall climbing routes. Stay right at all forks in the trail and keep going until you reach a huge left-facing dihedral with a chimney going up it. The thin crack about 10 feet left of the chimney is the start of The Great Zot (5.8+). Rewritten follows the flake system/arête to the left of that crack.

THE ROUTE:

Pitch 1: Take a look at The Great Zot crack—you'll be joining it at about 80 feet up. Start up the flakes to the left of The Great Zot, climbing carefully and taking care to place protection where you can. Follow a left-facing dihedral until it ends, then carefully move right into The Great Zot crack and follow it to the belay ledge.

Looking up Rebuffat's Arête on **Rewritten.** Photo by Mauricio Herrera Cuadra

Jack Sasser follows Pitch 5 of **Rewritten.** Photo by Brendan Leonard

A climber leads Pitch 4 of Rewritten.
Photo by Mauricio Herrera Cuadra

Pitch 2: Climb up and left on a flake through easier terrain to the Red Ledge, the huge shelf running left to right across the Redgarden Wall. Walk left on the Red Ledge to an eyebolt at the base of a huge left-facing corner.

Pitch 3: Climb up the corner on blocky terrain, through a narrow chimney, to a comfy niche in the corner. You'll see the hand traverse crack (the start of Pitch 4) heading left from this belay.

Pitch 4: Flip a coin or play rock-paper-scissors for this memorable lead. Place a piece off the belay and have another one handy, then hand traverse out left and smear your feet. At the end of the hand traverse, head up a beautiful, well-protected finger crack leading out left to the arête, and head around the arête into a corner. Place good gear in the corner (believe it or not, this is the crux of the pitch), and climb up to a ledge belay.

Pitch 5: From the belay, place a piece, step out onto Rebuffat's Arête above what feels like a mile of air, and head up. On this magical pitch, you'll find an incut hold along the arête right when you need it, and good gear on alternating sides of the sharp fin. The arête ends at a point—double up a cordelette or wrap sling around the point, clip yourself into the hanging stance, and bring up your partner.

Pitch 6: On the wall behind Rebuffat's Arête, climb the easy, short, right-angling crack to the top.

THE DESCENT: From the summit, walk north to a notch that drops to the west side of the wall (the side you climbed). Find the path down, which has a few easy 4th class moves. If you find yourself on something harder than 4th class, you're on the wrong descent route.

A topo of Rewritten. Photo by Dean Ronzoni

32. **Lover's Leap**

BY LEE SMITH

FORMATION	Lover's Leap
NUMBER OF PITCHES	3 pitches
RATING	5.7+
RACK	Standard rack
SEASON	Late spring to fall
SEASONAL CLOSURES	None known

COMMENT: Any rock climber traveling northbound on US 285 just west of Denver can't help but notice "The Leap" looming large above the highway and Turkey Creek. This soaring buttress on the lower flank of Mt. Lindo offers a great three-pitch adventure just minutes from downtown Denver. Straightforward route finding, ample protection, and a short steep approach combine to make this climb very popular. As on all great climbs, the crux of The Leap

Cindy Mitchell sends the crux of Lover's Leap. Photo by Jay Eggleston

is at the top of the route; the final headwall is steep, exposed, and very stout for its 5.7 rating. Northwest facing, Lover's Leap offers a cool climb on warmer days. The newly installed two-log bridge makes the climb accessible even during the high water days of spring.

Although it's gone now, for years the base of this climb had an old boot sitting on a ledge at the beginning of the route. "Is there a foot in it?" was the joking reply when your partner picked it up. The boot was a reminder of the seriousness of this climb. Several incidents, and even fatalities, have occurred at Lover's Leap. Due to road noise and the nature of the terrain, it's difficult to see or hear your partner, and a fall on the lower pitches would certainly lead to injury. Take this route seriously and have your communications system dialed.

A climber follows the second pitch. Photo by Lee Smith

GETTING THERE: From Denver, head west, aiming for southbound US 285 (Hampden Avenue). Lover's Leap is just over 3.0 miles from the junction of C-470 and US 285; however, you need to drive past it and make a U-turn 4.5 miles up the canyon at South Turkey Creek Road. Head back down US 285 and park at the pullout right below The Leap. Look up and carefully consider your future!

THE APPROACH: From the parking pullout, head down the steep bank to the two-log bridge over Turkey Creek. Follow the steep trail above a gully on the right and trend left under the face. Cross a couple of talus slopes. The trail leads straight to the base of the climb.

THE ROUTE:

Pitch 1: Beginning at the lowest point on the wall, head up through the blocky terrain trending right and following indistinct corner crack systems. Don't get suckered left; the terrain gets more difficult and less protectable. Find a great belay ledge 100 feet up and sling a block that looks surprisingly like a coffin.

Mike Morin on the two-log bridge. Photo by Lee Smith

Pitch 2: This is a long pitch so plan accordingly. Trending right, stem and jam up the blocky corner system always seeking the path of least resistance. Aim for the "Goal Post" silhouette on the horizon marking the exit headwall. Pitch 2 ends in a cave where you'll find a good two-bolt anchor.

Pitch 3: This is the reason you came. Traverse left around a small overhang and head back right to the headwall under the Goal Post. Try not to set up too much rope drag. Now the fun: head straight up the steep exposed headwall with great protection. Stem and jam your way up to the exit jugs and scramble straight ahead to a small tree with a two-bolt anchor. Exalt in your lofty position!

THE DESCENT: There are two options to get down. Three well-bolted rap stations head down into the western gully (climber's right) starting from the top anchor. A single 60-meter rope is fine for these, but be careful to pull your rope to avoid getting it stuck. Another descent is a walk off to the east around the buttress, skirting the base back to the trail.

Topo of Lover's Leap. Photo by Lee Smith

33. Chickenhead

BY LEE SMITH

FORMATION	The Headstone at Devil's Head
NUMBER OF PITCHES	3 pitches
RATING	5.8
RACK	Standard rack
SEASON	Spring to fall
SEASONAL CLOSURES	None known

COMMENT: A squeeze-job trad route among all the Devil's Head sport routes, Chickenhead was the first route up the imposing Headstone in the East Valley. Often ignored for some of the newer areas with easier access, the Headstone offers one of the longest climbs at Devil's Head. This route lives up to its name on the second pitch where climbers will find wave after wave of gargan-

Looking up the route from the base.
Photo by Lee Smith

Tracy Roach follows the first pitch.
Photo by Lee Smith

tuan chickenheads to pull on. In general, the protection is good, but the new leader must be wary of blocks being loose. Test your placements well and don't set cams in suspect cracks. Look around for natural protection opportunities—some of the chickenheads are big enough to throw a sling around.

Like most South Platte routes, Chickenhead gives climbers ample opportunity to test all their skills. You'll need to be comfortable with slab, stem, crack, and lieback techniques. The second pitch contains a very loose block that is hard to divert around—do not put any protection behind this block! Once you catch your breath after skirting the block, enjoy the heucos and chickenheads, as well as the airy exposure and incredible Devil's Head views. The west side of the Headstone is in the shade for half the day, so it can be climbed early on hot days and later on cool days. The belays are bolt protected, but the purists can build their own gear anchors if they choose.

GETTING THERE: From Denver, head south on Santa Fe Drive (US 85) to the town of Sedalia. Take a right on CO 67 and head west into the hills. After approximately 10 miles, take a blind left turn on Rampart Range Road. After 9.5 miles on Rampart Range Road, turn into the main parking lot for the Devil's Head Trail. This trailhead is very popular on summer weekends.

THE APPROACH: From the main trailhead parking, head up the fire tower trail—just follow the crowds. After a mile

Climber on the first pitch.
Photo by Tracy Roach

Climber rappelling the route.
Photo by Tracy Roach

or so, come to a fork in the trail. A small signpost points left to the Zinn Over-look—take this trail. The right fork heads to the fire tower. If you come to the fire tower, you've gone too far and missed the fork.

Once at the Zinn Overlook, head downhill and look carefully for a left fork in the faint trail. At this point you can see the Headstone. Follow the faint trail over some scrambly sections and head uphill to the base of the Headstone. If your bearings are correct, you meet the rock right at the base of Chickenhead.

THE ROUTE:

Pitch 1: Pitch 1 offers interesting climbing in a left-facing dihedral with plenty of protection. Stem, lieback, and smear your feet up the crack in the corner. Carefully look around for the best pro options, as well as the best holds. Trust those feet! Sometimes you'll need to reach above or behind you to find the best holds. The pitch ends up and right at a two-bolt anchor.

Pitch 2: This airy pitch will get your attention right off the belay. A short, exposed traverse left is difficult and awkward. Position your feet and body carefully and swing it up. The next obstacle is the aforementioned loose block (it's BIG). Best not to hang around here for too long. Cruise up the rest of the pitch in the chimney, or using the flakes, heucos, and chickenheads to the right. Avoid the loose blocks in the chimney by heading right. The next belay also has two bolts for an anchor, and it sits on a sloping ledge with an alarming view to the ground. Take some time to breathe again!

Pitch 3: There are two options: Stay in the chimney and grunge up the right side for a true trad climb, or use the bolts on the right face; this is the last pitch of Topaz, a sport route to the left of Chickenhead. Many parties forgo the short third pitch and rappel the route from the end of the second pitch.

THE DESCENT: As mentioned, many parties will rappel the route from the end of the second pitch. A 60-meter rope will reach the belay at the top of Pitch 1 and easily reach the ground from there. If you do the third pitch, rap the sport route Topaz, slightly to climber's left of Chickenhead.

Topo of Chickenhead. Photo by Lee Smith

34. Fun Climb 101

BY LEE SMITH

FORMATION	Ragnarok
NUMBER OF PITCHES	3 pitches
RATING	5.8+
RACK	Standard rack to 4 inches
SEASON	Late spring to fall
SEASONAL CLOSURES	None known

COMMENT: Ragnarok's Fun Climb 101 is the antonymic equivalent of calling the tall man "Shorty" and the big man "Tiny." It's far from a prerequisite class—and when pulling the burly lieback and mantle moves, it can feel less than fun. This route is one of the most difficult climbs in this book. The approach is long and tricky, involving mountain biking and a bushwhack with difficult route finding. The climbing route protects well, although some intimidating sections

Deb Roth on the third pitch. Photo by Ryan Wallace

require the climber to "go for it" and run it out. Climbers need to be well-educated on the whole South Platte bag of tricks for this one. Hand jams, slabby liebacks, difficult mantles, and reachy, in-your-face roof moves will challenge your abilities. You'll have to place protection on tenuous stances.

The approach to Ragnarok is best traveled on a mountain bike. Hiking it would add hours to the approach. The road is in good shape and trends uphill most of the way to Ragnarok, making for a quick descent back to the car. As always, be mindful of the afternoon thunderstorms that crop up quickly in the South Platte, and let someone know your plans, as this is a fairly remote climb. Most likely you'll have it all to yourselves.

In Norse mythology, Ragnarok refers to the Doom of the Gods. Apocalyptic

Brendan Leonard on the crux second pitch. Photo by Lee Smith

battles are fought and the cosmos is destroyed. Although this South Platte crag isn't quite as dramatic as the end of the world, climbers can find their own battles on this challenging route.

GETTING THERE: From Denver, take US 285 south to Pine Junction. At the stoplight, take a left (south) on S. Pine Valley Road. Continue past the towns of Pine and Buffalo Creek. Another 2.5 miles past Buffalo Creek, look for the gated Forest Service Road #538. Park here, making sure to not block the gate.

THE APPROACH: Jump on your bike and ride! FS Road #538 is a fairly well-maintained dirt road. Travel approximately 3.5 miles. After passing the junction with the Colorado Trail, look for an obvious closed and bermed road. Clamber over the berm, ditch the bikes, and begin the hike. Hike up this closed road a short distance keeping a sharp eye out for the formation called The Slabbo to your right (south). When the formation comes into view, head into the forest. Skirt the base of The Slabbo on the left (east) side and trend uphill passing another crag, The Cracked Wall. Finally, skirt (again on the left side) the Boulder Pile. The ultimate goal is a boulder-strewn gully between the Boulder Pile and Ragnarok. Travel right (west) up this gully, arriving at a notch between Ragn-

The authors biking to Ragnarok. Photo by Lee Smith

arok and the Boulder Pile. This saddle is where you want to rack up and leave your packs, as the descent will place you back at this point. Total hiking distance to the saddle is approximately 0.75 mile. After enjoying the view, head down the gully to the west and skirt the base of Ragnarok. Fun Climb 101 is an obvious dihedral on the eastern side of Ragnarok. Congratulate yourself for making it this far.

THE ROUTE:
Pitch 1: Start in the obvious corner with some easy and well-protected face climbing. At a roof, head left and grovel/lieback up a wide crack/fin system. Belay at a ledge with a large block to sling.

Pitch 2: Bring out your hero moves: Liebacking with slabby feet, hand jamming, and an in-your-face move around a roof with a big reach to your left. The pitch culminates in a difficult mantle move. Belay at a big ledge and breathe a sigh of relief.

Pitch 3: Look left from the belay and locate a nice splitter. Climb it! Continue up and right over blocky terrain aiming for a big notch that marks the summit. Keep your rope as straight as possible to mitigate drag. Enjoy the view.

THE DESCENT: From the top, look for the saddle between Ragnarok and the Boulder Pile. Head northerly and downclimb the blocky boulders to the saddle. Careful route finding should keep this at 4th class.

Topo of Fun Climb 101. Photo by Lee Smith

35. The Staircase

BY BRENDAN LEONARD

FORMATION	Arch Rock
NUMBER OF PITCHES	2-3 pitches
RATING	5.5
RACK	Standard rack
SEASON	Spring to fall
SEASONAL CLOSURES	None known

COMMENT: The granite in Elevenmile Canyon is overlooked by many climbers living near Denver, Fort Collins, and Boulder—it's a two-and-one-half-hour drive to get there from Denver, which is tough to justify for a day trip, but worth it for a weekend or longer (and can even be worth it for a day trip if you're motivated to get in enough pitches). The mix of bolted and trad climbs lining the domes and crags in Elevenmile is more plentiful than online resources suggest,

Arch Rock. Photo by Brendan Leonard

and there are lines from one to four pitches on the faces scattered along the creek cutting through the middle of the canyon. At about 8,200 feet and higher, Elevenmile Canyon is a couple thousand feet higher than many of the climbs in this book, so the season can be a bit shorter—late April to mid-November, depending on snow levels.

The Staircase is a great climb for new trad leaders, but also a fun intro to Elevenmile for climbers of any grade. It climbs solid granite to the top of Arch Rock, eats up any gear you want to place in it (especially nuts), has plenty of rests, and has spacious belay ledges. That, of course, means it's popular, so get to the base of the climb early and climb it before the crowds show up, and leave plenty of time to spend the rest of your day exploring some of the other Elevenmile classics in this book.

The start of Staircase. The route heads up the right-facing dihedral.
Photo by Brendan Leonard

GETTING THERE: From Denver, drive south on I-25 to Colorado Springs, and take Exit 141 onto US 24, heading west toward Woodland Park. Approximately 20 miles past Woodland Park, at the town of Lake George, turn left (south) onto Park County Road 96 and drive to the Elevenmile Canyon State Park entrance station and pay the entry fee. Continue on County Road 96 into the park, keeping an eye out for Arch Rock on your left, about 4.0 miles after the entrance station. Park in a pullout near the base of the rock.

THE APPROACH: Depending on your parking spot, find one of the approach trails on the east side of the road and grunt up the short hike through the trees to the west face, making your way to the northern half of the rock and the big right-facing dihedral where The Staircase begins.

THE ROUTE:

Pitch 1: Head up the dihedral, following cracks and placing gear at will—this is a great pitch for newer leaders to sew it up. At about 50 feet, a nice ledge on the left side of the dihedral and beneath a big roof makes for a great belay.

Hilary Oliver leads Pitch 1 of Staircase. Photo by Brendan Leonard

Pitch 2: (Pitches 1 and 2 can easily be combined.) Continue into the second, steeper part of the dihedral, past a series of "ribs" (the actual "Staircase") on the left side of the corner. Just above the staircase and below a steep, wide crack, build a belay on a big ledge out left. If you can, make your way as far left as you can before building your belay. The third pitch goes up easy rock to the left of your original dihedral, so you'll have rope drag belaying your second on this pitch, or leading the last pitch, or both—depending where you set up your belay.

Pitch 3: From the belay, step left, then climb a face and then a crack system up and right to the summit.

THE DESCENT: Walk off the top of the formation to the south, trending around to the west face and returning to the base of the climb to grab your gear.

A route topo of Staircase. Photo by Brendan Leonard

36. Jaws

BY BRENDAN LEONARD

FORMATION	Turret Dome
NUMBER OF PITCHES	3-4 pitches
RATING	5.7/5.7+
RACK	Standard rack to #4 Camalot, with plenty of long slings
SEASON	Spring to fall
SEASONAL CLOSURES	None known

COMMENT: Jaws is a classic route to the summit of Turret Dome, with fantastic second and third pitches that require vastly different climbing. The undercling traverse on the second pitch is fun and interesting for the grade, and requires some strategic gear placement to avoid heinous rope drag. Climbers have two options to finish the route, which also are the options to finish the adjacent climb, Schooldaze, so if you're climbing both routes (easily doable in a day), pick one finish for Jaws and try the other one when you climb Schooldaze.

Hilary Oliver follows Pitch 2 of Jaws. Photo by Brendan Leonard

GETTING THERE: From Denver, drive south on I-25 to Colorado Springs, and take Exit 141 onto US 24, heading west toward Woodland Park. Approximately 20 miles past Woodland Park, at the town of Lake George, turn left (south) onto Park County Road 96 and drive to the Elevenmile Canyon State Park entrance station and pay the entry fee. Continue on County Road 96 into the park until you see a large parking lot with restrooms and a footbridge crossing the creek, about 4.0 miles from the park entrance section—this is where you'll park, but it's not a bad idea to drive another half mile down the road and scope out the face of Turret Dome to check out the routes. Jaws climbs the right side of a huge arch on the south side of Turret Dome.

THE APPROACH: From the parking lot, cross the footbridge and look for a trail heading left parallel to the creek. Follow the trail for about 800 feet until it disappears in the talus at the base of Turret Dome. Scramble up and left, contouring around the face of the rock, until you arrive at a gully with a pine tree growing out of its right-hand wall. The first pitch of Jaws climbs the featured, easy rock at the back of the gully.

THE ROUTE:

Pitch 1: Climb the easy rock at the back of the gully (5.3/5.4), and at the top, head right and up to belay at a small tree.

Pitch 2: Head up from the tree belay into the sweeping crack above your head. Place a piece in the crack and, since you'll be traversing left the rest of this pitch, put a long sling on it to mitigate rope drag. It will also help if you place your first piece as far left as you can. Continue traversing

The start of Jaws. The first pitch begins up the wall to the climber's left in this photo.
Photo by Hilary Oliver

The "bathtubs" on Pitch 3 of Jaws.
Photo by Brendan Leonard

Jaws has two finishes: The splitter crack on the right is easier, and the left-angling crack to its left is much more difficult. Photo by Brendan Leonard

left, taking advantage of opportunities to place pro where you can. You've probably only got one big piece (#4 or #5) with you, so try to use your smaller gear first. As you traverse left and undercling the roof, the crack gets bigger and bigger. Keep your weight on your feet as the handholds run out and you round the corner to follow the top of the arch. Traverse to the right-facing dihedral, place a piece, and pull over the dihedral to belay under a roof.

Pitch 3: Head up easy ground to "the bathtubs," placing gear when you can, and have fun climbing up the huge holes in the rock where good gear is sparse, but the climbing is easy. Climb past the top of the bathtubs to belay under a big roof with a perfect fist crack splitting it.

Pitch 4: Choose from two options here: Option 1 heads straight up the splitter fist crack (5.6) and follows it as it leans back to horizontal. It ends at the base of a short dihedral heading to the summit, which has one stout 5.7 move and then easier climbing to the summit. Option 2 is a hand crack about 30 feet left of the belay, which climbs over a lip and might feel like one of the tougher 5.7+ moves you've done. Plug in a #3 Camalot and go for it, then continue up to the summit.

THE DESCENT: Walk northwest towards the back side of Turret Dome, and scramble and downclimb into a short gully with a 40-foot rappel. Many parties downclimb this steep section, but many also rappel off a chockstone in the gully. After the rappel or downclimb, head right and down slabs to easy ground and a faint trail back down to the footbridge to the parking lot.

A route topo of Jaws. Photo by Brendan Leonard

37. Schooldaze

BY BRENDAN LEONARD

FORMATION	Turret Dome
NUMBER OF PITCHES	3-4 pitches
RATING	5.7/5.7+
RACK	Standard rack to #4 Camalot, with plenty of long slings
SEASON	Spring to fall
SEASONAL CLOSURES	None known

COMMENT: Schooldaze is one of many fun multi-pitch routes on Turret Dome—laid-back granite with varied trad climbing techniques, starting up an off-width-size crack (that doesn't require any off-width technique!), then climbing huge hueco "bathtubs" to one of two crack finishes to the Turret Dome summit. Climbers have two options to finish the route, which also are the options to finish the adjacent climb, Jaws, so if you're climbing both routes (easily doable in a day), pick one finish for Schooldaze and try the other one when you climb Jaws.

The start of Schooldaze. The route begins up the grassy dihedral in the center of the photo and continues up the right-facing corner above. Photo by Brendan Leonard

Hilary Oliver follows Pitch 2 of Schooldaze. Photo by Brendan Leonard

GETTING THERE: From Denver, drive south on I-25 to Colorado Springs, and take Exit 141 onto US 24, heading west toward Woodland Park. Approximately 20 miles past Woodland Park, at the town of Lake George, turn left (south) onto Park County Road 96 and drive to the Elevenmile Canyon State Park entrance station and pay the entry fee. Continue on County Road 96 into the park until you see a large parking lot with restrooms and a footbridge crossing the creek, about 4.0 miles from the park entrance section—this is where you'll park, but it's not a bad idea to drive another half mile down the road and scope out the face of Turret Dome to check out the routes. Schooldaze starts up a huge left-facing dihedral that forms the left side of a huge arch on the south side of Turret Dome.

THE APPROACH: From the parking lot, cross the footbridge and look for a trail heading left parallel to the creek. Follow the trail for about 800 feet until it disappears in the talus at the base of Turret Dome. Scramble up and left, contouring around the face of the rock, until you arrive at the base of a huge, laid-back, left-facing dihedral that goes up into a right-facing dihedral above. This is the start of the route.

THE ROUTE:

Pitch 1 and 2: Climb the easy left-facing dihedral to its transition into the right-facing dihedral, where the wideness starts. As you start to climb up the right-facing dihedral, consider stopping to belay to mitigate rope drag. If you have a 70-meter rope, you can climb all the way to a belay at the top of the arch, but rope drag may be a big issue. As you climb, stay close to the dihedral and when you see a chance to place gear, take it—it's wide, and you'll probably only have one big piece with you, so use it wisely. Plenty of good gear can be found in the dihedral if you wiggle your way back in there, and a few pieces can be plugged into cracks along the way. When you near the top of the arch, either build a belay under the big roof, or pull over the dihedral to the left and build a belay just left of the top of the arch.

Pitch 3: Head up easy ground to "the bathtubs," placing gear when you can, and have fun climbing up the huge holes in the rock where good gear is sparse, but the climbing is easy. Climb past the top of the bathtubs to belay under a big roof with a perfect fist crack splitting it.

Pitch 4: Choose from two options here: Option 1 heads straight up the splitter fist crack (5.6) and follows it as it leans back to horizontal. It ends at the base of a short dihedral heading to the summit, which has one stout 5.7 move and then easier climbing to the summit. Option 2 is a hand crack about 30 feet left of the belay, which climbs over a lip and might feel like one of the tougher 5.7+ moves you've done. Plug in a #3 Camalot and go for it, then continue up to the summit.

THE DESCENT: Walk northwest towards the back side of Turret Dome, and scramble and downclimb into a short gully with a 40-foot rappel. Many parties downclimb this steep section, but many also rappel off a chockstone in the gully. After the rappel or downclimb, head right and down slabs to easy ground and a faint trail back down to the footbridge to the parking lot.

A route topo of Schooldaze. Photo by Brendan Leonard

38. Guide's Route

BY BRENDAN LEONARD

FORMATION	Turret Dome
NUMBER OF PITCHES	3-4 pitches
RATING	5.6
RACK	Standard rack to #3 Camalot, with plenty of long slings
SEASON	Spring to fall
SEASONAL CLOSURES	None known

COMMENT: Guide's Route is a fun adventure climb to the summit of Turret Dome, the largest rock in Elevenmile Canyon. Many possible variations exist for its second and third pitches—we'll describe just one here, but know that it's possible to follow your nose and find your own way to the summit after the first pitch. The steeper first pitch is the crux of the route, followed by a few heady slab moves on the second pitch. The route name refers to climbing guides' long-

Brendan Leonard leads Pitch 2 of Guide's Route. Photo by Hilary Oliver

Guide's Route starts up the twin cracks between the trees. Photo by Brendan Leonard

time use of this route to take clients to the top of Turret Dome and enjoy the view from the summit.

GETTING THERE: From Denver, drive south on I-25 to Colorado Springs, and take Exit 141 onto US 24, heading west toward Woodland Park. Approximately 20 miles past Woodland Park at the town of Lake George, turn left (south) onto Park County Road 96 and drive to the Elevenmile Canyon State Park entrance station and pay the entry fee. Continue on County Road 96 into the park until you see a large parking lot with restrooms and a footbridge crossing the creek, about 4.0 miles from the park entrance section—this is where you'll park, but it's not a bad idea to drive another half mile down the road and scope out the face of Turret Dome to check out the routes. Guide's Route lies in an alcove about 200 feet left and uphill from the huge arch on the south face of Turret Dome.

THE APPROACH: From the parking lot, cross the footbridge and look for a trail heading left parallel to the creek. Follow the trail for about 800 feet until it disappears in the talus at the base of Turret Dome. Scramble up and left, contouring around the face of the rock, past the huge arch on the south face, until you

Brendan Leonard leads Pitch 3 of Guide's Route.

Photo by Hilary Oliver

arrive at a small alcove between two tall pine trees at a wall with three parallel cracks.

THE ROUTE:

Pitch 1: Begin up the left of the three parallel cracks and plug in gear until you see a fixed piton at about 45 feet (this is the crux)—pull over it and step right to join the right-hand crack and follow it until it mellows out. Build a belay just below a roof that ends at a left-facing dihedral.

Pitch 2: From the belay, climb next to the left-facing dihedral on face holds, and then head up and right on runout, but easy climbing in the "bathtub" huecos, aiming for an overhang at the left edge of the bathtubs where you'll find a three-piton anchor.

Pitch 3: Here's where your long slings will come in handy: Head up and right from the belay and route-find, weaving through a bunch of flakes and rooflets until the climbing eases to the summit. This pitch can feel like several easy boulder problems alternated with easy scrambling. If the rope drag becomes too much, just find a decent ledge, plug in some gear, and split this last pitch in two—yes, adding another pitch will take longer, but you might stay a little more sane by skipping the rope-hauling.

THE DESCENT: Walk northwest towards the back side of Turret Dome, and scramble and downclimb into a short gully with a 40-foot rappel. Many parties downclimb this steep section, but many also rappel off a chockstone in the gully. After the rappel or downclimb, head right and down slabs to easy ground and a faint trail back down to the footbridge to the parking lot.

A topo of Guide's Route. Photo by Brendan Leonard

39. North Ridge

BY BRENDAN LEONARD

FORMATION	Montezuma Tower
NUMBER OF PITCHES	2 pitches
RATING	5.7
RACK	Single set of cams, a double-length sling, and an extra rope for rappelling
SEASON	Year round, depending on snow cover
SEASONAL CLOSURES	None known

COMMENT: Montezuma Tower is one of the funkiest summits accessible from the Front Range—a thin red sandstone blade sticking straight up out of the foothills below the famous Pikes Peak. It looks like something that might have been plucked out of the Utah desert and dropped into Garden of the Gods, a city park at the west edge of Colorado Springs.

Montezuma Tower. Photo by Brendan Leonard

A climber leads Pitch 1 of the North Ridge. Photo by Brendan Leonard

Montezuma Tower isn't exactly a wilderness climb—you'll be among plenty of tourists as you walk the flat sidewalk to the base of the route, and you'll be on center stage above them as soon as you start this two-pitch classic. The North Ridge climbs Montezuma Tower's narrow spine, exposed on all sides except right in front of your face—a unique position that makes a fall off either side feel like a scary possibility. The climbing is mostly 5.6 after the opening moves. Near the top, the ridge narrows to the point that you can straddle it as if you're riding horseback 120 feet off the ground. Expect peanut gallery commentary, and cheers and waves from the folks on the ground below.

U.S. Army climbers first summitted Montezuma Tower via this route in the '50s, likely using points of aid on driven pitons, and Harvey Carter came along and free climbed the route in the 1960s.

If you haven't filled out a climbing permit for the current year, head to the Garden of the Gods visitor center and complete one before your climb. If it's rained the day or the night before, don't climb at Garden of the Gods—the sandstone is especially weak when it's wet.

GETTING THERE: From Denver, drive to Colorado Springs on I-25. Take the Garden of the Gods Road exit and drive west on Garden of the Gods Road to its intersection with 30th Street. Turn left onto 30th Street and follow it south to the

Hilary Oliver follows Pitch 1 of the North Ridge. Photo by Brendan Leonard

Garden of the Gods park entrance. Drive into Garden of the Gods and follow the loop road to the main parking lot (the first large parking lot on your left).

THE APPROACH: This might be one of the easiest approach "hikes" in this book—it's almost completely flat. Walk south on the sidewalks between the Gateway Rocks and past the Twin Spires. Montezuma Tower is the prominent thin red sandstone tower to the south. Leave the sidewalk and walk south to the bottom of its north ridge and flake your rope.

THE ROUTE:

Pitch 1: The crux of this route might be the bouldery start right off the ground— a large block fell off the start several years ago and makes it a little less straightforward. Head straight up the ridge, plugging in pro where you can and clipping the three enormous ring bolts. At least one good piece of pro can be built by girth-hitching a double-length sling through a pothole in the sandstone on your way up. This pitch will require a couple moves on dishes that get smoother every year—trust friction, and concentrate on standing up slowly and controlled on your shoe rubber. Belay at a ledge with fixed pitons.

Pitch 2: The second pitch has one steep 5.7 crack move and then the angle relents and you're on top of the ridge. Belay at a two-bolt anchor, enjoy the view from the top, and pose for some photos.

THE DESCENT: Tie two ropes together for the just-barely-over 35-meter rappel down the west side of the tower.

A route topo of the North Ridge. Photo by Brendan Leonard

40. New Era

BY BRENDAN LEONARD

FORMATION	Grey Rock
NUMBER OF PITCHES	3 pitches
RATING	5.7
RACK	Standard rack
SEASON	Year round, depending on snow
SEASONAL CLOSURES	None known

COMMENT: New Era is a classic Garden of the Gods route, put up in 1959 by Harvey Carter, hardman and legendary founder of *Climbing* magazine. Many climbers do only the first two pitches of this climb (often linked as one long pitch) and then rappel off the anchors at the top of the second pitch. It's a fair practice, as there are a number of interesting trad and sport routes neighboring New Era—but for the purposes of this book, we'll continue to the south summit

Grey Rock. Photo by Brendan Leonard

The route follows the obvious obtuse dihedral in the center of the photo. Photo by Brendan Leonard

of Grey Rock as the late Mr. Carter did half a century ago. You might find the old school 5.7 rating on this one a bit stout, especially at the layback section at the top of the second pitch.

If you're uncomfortable downclimbing exposed 4th class terrain, be warned that the descent down Grey Rock's east ridge involves a healthy amount of technical moves on the way. Downclimbing is a skill every climber should have, and the descent off Grey Rock is a great place to practice that skill. Find good footholds, stay in control, and don't get in a hurry.

GETTING THERE: From Denver, drive to Colorado Springs on I-25. Take the Garden of the Gods Road exit and drive west on Garden of the Gods Road to its intersection with 30th Street. Turn left onto 30th Street and follow it south to the Garden of the Gods park entrance. Drive into Garden of the Gods and, on your way in, study the broad grey formation straight ahead of you. Look for a prominent dihedral on the east side of the left (south) of the two summits. New Era climbs the rock to the left of that dihedral. Follow the loop road almost all the way around in a circle to the south parking lot, at the top of a hill looking at the south face of Grey Rock.

THE APPROACH: Walk down the road towards Grey Rock, looking for an obvious climbers' trail leading up the steep hillside to the east face of the formation. New Era begins directly under the left-facing, open-book dihedral.

THE ROUTE:

Pitch 1: Climb jugs and flakes toward the dihedral, stopping to belay at a piton anchor about 75 feet up. The advantage of setting up a belay here is that the leader has a full rack for the crux of the route (the stem or layback section on the next pitch), but the disadvantage is the hanging/slightly uncomfortable nature of the belay. If you're feeling strong and confident, go for it. Linking the pitches makes for one long, 160-foot pitch.

Chris El-Deiry follows Pitch 2 of New Era. Photo by Brendan Leonard

Hilary Oliver follows Pitch 1 of New Era.
Photo by Brendan Leonard

Chris El-Deiry leads Pitch 3 of New Era.
Photo by Brendan Leonard

Pitch 2: From the fixed pins, continue up the crack to where the right wall of the dihedral becomes smooth. Place a piece of gear and either stem your feet out on the walls and hand jam the crack, or place your feet on the left wall and layback the short crux. After the crux, belay at a four-pin belay station in a cave. If you're uncomfortable with pigeon excrement, you're not going to be excited about this belay—the cave is usually well painted with it.

Pitch 3: Step out of the cave to the right and pull up on flakes on exposed (but only 5.4) terrain and continue up the arête to the summit.

THE DESCENT: Backpack coil your rope and scramble down the south ridge of Grey Rock on 4th class rock, starting in chimneys and eventually ending on a friction slab/ramp at the southeast corner of the formation.

A route topo of New Era. Photo by Brendan Leonard

About the Authors

Brendan Leonard is the creator of Semi-Rad.com; a contributing editor at *Climbing, Adventure Journal*, and *The Dirtbag Diaries*; and has climbed trad routes throughout the Front Range and the West since Lee Smith taught him how to place gear in 2007.

Lee Smith is a longtime climber, mountaineer, and alpine lover. He's been ascending mountains and crags for more than 40 years and hopes someday to be an accomplished climber. Recruited by co-conspirator Brendan Leonard for this guidebook, Lee dusted off his ancient degree in journalism and learned how to spell again. When he's not engaged in his career as an aircraft maintenance technician, Lee will likely be found hanging off some remote precipice.

Checklist of Climbing Routes by Grade

GRADE		ROUTE	NUMBER	PAGE	DATE/NOTE
	☐	**Rock One Route**, Rock One, *LUMPY RIDGE*	#1	20	
5.4	☐	**Standard East Face**, Third Flatiron, *FLATIRONS*	#17	84	
	☐	**North Arête**, First Flatiron, *FLATIRONS*	#18	88	
5.4 R	☐	**East Face North Side**, Seal Rock, *FLATIRONS*	#19	92	
	☐	**East Face North Side**, Fifth Flatiron, *FLATIRONS*	#20	96	
	☐	**Fandango**, First Flatiron, *FLATIRONS*	#22	104	
	☐	**Tigger**, Wind Tower, *ELDORADO CANYON*	#26	120	
5.5	☐	**Swanson Arête**, Redgarden Wall, *ELDORADO CANYON*	#27	124	
	☐	**The Staircase**, Arch Rock, *ELEVENMILE CANYON*	#35	156	
5.5 R	☐	**East Face**, The Fatiron, *FLATIRONS*	#21	100	
	☐	**Batman and Robin**, Batman Pinnacle, *LUMPY RIDGE*	#2	24	
	☐	**Right Standard**, McGregor Slab, *FALL RIVER VALLEY*	#9	52	
5.6	☐	**The North Face**, The Matron, *FLATIRONS*	#25	116	
	☐	**Guide's Route**, Turret Dome, *ELEVENMILE CANYON*	#38	168	
5.6 R	☐	**Direct East Face**, First Flatiron, *FLATIRONS*	#23	108	
	☐	**The North Face**, The Maiden, *FLATIRONS*	#24	112	
	☐	**Magical Chrome-Plated Semi-Automatic Enema Syringe**, The Pear, *LUMPY RIDGE*	#3	28	
	☐	**White Whale**, Left Book, *LUMPY RIDGE*	#5	36	
	☐	**The Ridge**, Piz Badille, *SOUTH ST. VRAIN*	#10	56	
	☐	**North Face Center**, Cob Rock, *BOULDER CANYON*	#13	68	
5.7	☐	**Wind Ridge**, Wind Tower, *ELDORADO CANYON*	#28	128	
	☐	**Recon to West Overhang**, Wind Tower, *ELDORADO CANYON*	#29	132	
	☐	**Rewritten**, Redgarden Wall, *ELDORADO CANYON*	#31	140	
	☐	**North Ridge**, Montezuma Tower, *GARDEN OF THE GODS*	#39	172	
	☐	**New Era**, Grey Rock, *GARDEN OF THE GODS*	#40	176	

GRADE		ROUTE	NUMBER	PAGE	DATE/NOTE
5.7+	☐	**Cozyhang**, The Dome, *BOULDER CANYON*	#11	60	
	☐	**The Owl**, The Dome, *BOULDER CANYON*	#12	64	
	☐	**Empor**, Cob Rock, *BOULDER CANYON*	#14	72	
	☐	**Bastille Crack**, The Bastille, *ELDORADO CANYON*	#30	136	
	☐	**Lover's Leap**, Lover's Leap, *MT. LINDO*	#32	144	
	☐	**Jaws**, Turret Dome, *ELEVENMILE CANYON*	#36	160	
	☐	**Schooldaze**, Turret Dome, *ELEVENMILE CANYON*	#37	164	
5.8	☐	**Kor's Flake**, Sundance Buttress, *LUMPY RIDGE*	#4	32	
	☐	**The 37ᵗʰ Cog in Melvin's Wheel**, The Bookmark, *LUMPY RIDGE*	#7	44	
	☐	**Nun's Buttress**, Deer Mountain, *FALL RIVER VALLEY*	#8	48	
	☐	**Northwest Corner**, Cob Rock, *BOULDER CANYON*	#15	76	
	☐	**Chickenhead**, The Headstone at Devil's Head, *SOUTH PLATTE*	#33	148	
5.8+	☐	**Pear Buttress**, The Book, *LUMPY RIDGE*	#6	40	
	☐	**Bitty Buttress**, Blob Rock Massif, *BOULDER CANYON*	#16	80	
	☐	**Fun Climb 101**, Ragnarok, *SOUTH PLATTE*	#34	152	

Get Outside.

Become a CMC Member, today!

Explore the mountains and meet new people with the Colorado Mountain Club. Join us for trips, hikes, and activities throughout the state! Join today and save with special membership promotions for our readers: www.cmc.org/readerspecials

The Colorado Mountain Club is the state's leading organization dedicated to adventure, recreation, conservation, and education. Founded in 1912, the CMC acts as a gateway to the mountains for novices and experts alike, offering an array of year-round activities, events, and schools centered on outdoor recreation.

When you join the Colorado Mountain Club, you receive a variety of member benefits including:

- 20% member discount on CMC Press books
- 15% member discount on CMC hats, t-shirts, and hoodies
- 40% off admission to the American Mountaineering Museum
- Discounts at various outdoor retailers
- 4 issues of *Trail & Timberline* magazine
- FREE signups to over 3,000 mountain adventures annually
- Access to courses, classes, and seminars throughout the state
- Adventure Travel opportunities to take you to the world's great destinations